Here Lies
LALO

The Collected Poems of
ABELARDO DELGADO

Here Lies
LALO

The Collected Poems of
ABELARDO DELGADO

EDITED, WITH AN INTRODUCTION, BY

JARICA LINN WATTS

FOREWORD BY ARTURO J. ALDAMA

Here Lies Lalo: The Collected Poems of Abelardo Delgado is made possible through grants from the City of Houston through the Houston Arts Alliance.

Recovering the past, creating the future

Arte Público Press
University of Houston
452 Cullen Performance Hall
Houston, Texas 77204-2004

Cover design by Pilar Espino
Cover photo courtesy of Arte Público Press archives

Abelardo, 1931-2004.
 [Poems. English & Spanish. Selections]
 Here Lies Lalo : The Collected Poems of Abelardo Delgado /
Edited, with an introduction, by Jarica Linn Watts; prefatory note
by Dolores Huerta; foreword by Arturo J. Aldama.
   p. cm.
Includes bibliographical references and index.
ISBN 978-1-55885-694-3 (alk. paper)
 1. Mexican Americans—Poetry. I. Watts, Jarica Linn. II. Title.
PS3551.B3375A6 2011
811'.54—dc22   2010054400
                                                          CIP

♾ The paper used in this publication meets the requirements of the American National Standard for Information Sciences—Permanence of Paper for Printed Library Materials, ANSI Z39.48-1984.

11 12 13 14 15 16 17   10 9 8 7 6 5 4 3 2 1

TABLE OF CONTENTS

*Also published in *Under the Skirt of Lady Justice*.

BAJO EL SOL DE AZTLÁN (1973)

*Also published in *Under the Skirt of Lady Justice*.

UNDER THE SKIRT OF LADY JUSTICE: 43 SKIRTS OF ABELARDO (1978)

Special thanks to Vince Cheng,
Jim Allen and the Delgado family.

For my parents and Jessi Rose.

For Clint and my Saylor, whose scribbles
dot every draft of this project.

PREFATORY NOTE

LALO DELGADO'S POETRY GAVE WORDS TO THE LIFE AND SUFFERING OF THE farmworkers, Chicanos, Mexicanos in an irreverent, artful often humorous voice. His life's experience in the Southwest covered the human landscape of social survival by the oppressed and their activism to make changes. He shines a clear poetic light to identify the specific issues that cause pain and discrimination by those that are unaware of how their actions hurt others.

Lalo always leaves the reader with hope and love; by reading his poetry and shared wisdom one is not only educated but uplifted.

—*Dolores Huerta*

FOREWORD

Abelardo Lalo Delgado
Que en paz descanse

A CHICANA AND CHICANO CULTURAL AND LITERARY RENAISSANCE OPENED A vibrancy of literary, performative and visual empowerment that went hand in hand with the Chicano movement for social justice, equal rights and struggles for farm worker, educational and political empowerment. Denver and Colorado serve as a nexus point of the Chicana and Chicano movement, where artists, activists, students, families and workers rose up and said *ya basta* to institutionalized practices that degrade the cultural pluracy of Chicanas and Chicanos and all those of Mexican descent in the United States. Lalo Delgado, having immigrated here from northern Mexico, felt first-hand the rule of Ango-centrism race and class oppression, segregation, poverty and discrimination based on language, skin color, national origin and cultural difference. Lalo, rather than allowing his inner voice to become humiliated and sterilized by the imposition of monolingual hegemonies, spoke back, wrote back and celebrated his borderland identity, and articulated his deep felt convictions in the power of solidarity and group struggle and the power of collective cultural *dignidad*. Miriam Bornstein-Somoza's article, "Pedagogical Practices of Liberation in Abelardo 'Lalo' Delgado's Movement Poetry,"[1] looks at Lalo's poetic corpus of fourteen published works to argue that his poetic discourse contributes to an active pedagogy

---

[1]See Miriam Bornstein-Somoza, "Pedagogical Practices of Liberation in Abelardo 'Lalo' Delgado's Movement Poetry" Ed. Aldama, Facio, Maeda, Rabaka, *Enduring Legacies of the Colorado Borderlands* (Boulder: UP of Colorado, 2011). 327–345.

of oppressed Chicana/o peoples. Specifically, Bornstein-Somoza argues that in Delgado's poetic discourse:

> Chicanos/as become subjects of their particular historical moment as relations between dominant and marginalized or subaltern communities are altered. He does not expect the dominant culture to authorize him since he authorizes himself in order to create a voice that gives meaning to the representative function of the word. (222)

In having Chicanas/os become subjects of their historic moment and agents of our language, Delgado takes seriously the artistic legacies of Mesoamerica, and enters in the Xochitl Cuicatl flor y canto (flower and song) traditions of the Aztec or Mexica past, bringing them into a heteroglossic neocolonial present. His poetry reflects the indigeneity of Chicanas and Chicanos, and honors the struggle for cultural and linguistic pluralities of the US and México borderlands. His impressive corpus of published work plays a central role to what poet and theorist Alfred Arteaga calls poetic language of the Chicana and Chicano community[2]:

> Language itself, the very fabric of the poem, is significant in the delineation of the homeland and its people. Poetic language is particularly to the task of myth, to envisioning a national origin, and to the tasks of defining a people, their place on the planet, and their future. (17)

On a personal note, when I was asked to write this foreword, I was deeply humbled and in awe of how one human being and his infectious struggle to have a voice has touched the lives of generations of people in all walks of life, from young children to elders. He is remembered as a gentle spirit who was driven by indomitable kindness and a militant *respeto* for the unique creative potential of every person he interacted with. He is remembered for being a selfless and truly organic intellectual, and a fighter for the creative and educational rights of a community that continues to stand against an entrenched and ongoing system of intentional disenfranchisement. Helen

---

[2]See Alfred Arteaga, *Chicano Poetics: Heterotexts and Hybridities* (Cambridge UP, 1997). 17.

Girón, a Chicano Studies professor at Denver Metro and longtime commu-
nity activist and close friend of Lalo's for over 20 years, remembers his
charisma and community-building spirit: ". . . as a young girl (23 or so) I
worked for the United Farm Workers Union here in Denver for $5 a week.
Many times the picket lines were attacked by the Klan. . . . This always
made me so fearful. However, when I watched Lalo speak or take on issues,
and how to be courageous even in the darkest moments, it gave me the
strength to continue on the picket lines and even face arrest."

The poem below written at Lalo's funeral and public mourning cere-
mony by another longtime *compañero* also gives testimony to Lalo whom
he calls the "humble poet laureate de Aztlán" and the "grandfather to gen-
erations of Chicano poets who dared to pick up the pen."

LALO'S VELORIO

Here lies *Don Abelardo Delgado*
humble poet laureate *de Aztlán*
a hero to those who till the soil
trabajadores whose hands
have become warped and decrypted
making *masa* made of *tierra*
for *los ricos de América.* Lalo
freedom fighter for *los de abajo*
grandfather to the generations
of Chicano poets who dared to pick up
the pen, crafting images *de una vida dura*
pero también llena de esperanza.

—*Ramón del Castillo*
Chair of Chicana and Chicano Studies,
Metropolitan State College, Denver, CO

In conclusion: His physical body might be gone, his spirit has journeyed to
Mictlán, yet the body of his poetic spirit lives on in the communal memory
of *la gente.*

Please read the following book, be inspired, challenged and mesmer-
ized, and gain courage to fight for your creative truths.

INTRODUCTION

ABELARDO "LALO" DELGADO WAS TWELVE YEARS OLD WHEN HE EMIGRATED from Chihuahua, Mexico, to El Paso, Texas. He was alone with his mother, and the year was 1943. As a Mexican student in an American school system that forbade him to speak the only language he knew, Delgado launched his first organized protest: he refused to stand for the singing of America's national anthem, insisting, instead, that his classmates join *him* in singing the *Himno Nacional Mexicano*. One week later, his sixth-grade class was singing *vivas* to Mexico. His mother raised him in a public housing complex with 23 other families, and he stayed put just long enough to graduate from Bowie High School as Vice President of the Honor Society. He then worked with troubled and impoverished youth, and eventually found his way to the University of Texas at El Paso in 1962.

From there, his story is legendary. There's the part where, during his engagement, he sent his wife a poem—accompanied by a dollar bill—*every day*, for a few months: "with this, you buy a wedding dress,"[1] the inscription read every time. Or the part where he was recruited—by an Irishman, no less!—to lobby on behalf of Mexican migrant farm workers. The part where he gave César Chávez some unsolicited advice and later, after seeing Chávez lose forty-thousand dollars because of that very advice, recanted his recommendation: "Don't listen to me anymore, Chávez. I'm crazy."[2] But, for the story the history books will later tell, these small details matter not. For Lalo Delgado was decidedly important. After all, there is the part where he picked up a pen and began to write about the plight of Mexican Americans

---

[1] Delgado, Abelardo. Interview with Lisa Olken of Rocky Mountain PBS Television. "La Raza de Colorado." Rocky Mountain PBS Television, June 2005.
[2] Ibid.

—and, in so doing, set the foundation for Chicano letters and literature. He wanted, he said, to use his words "as a platform to identify the hurt." He wanted to "preserve [his] culture."[3] He wanted to inspire the movement—as he called it, "the vast movement for total change." And in this regard, he was successful: upon his death in 2004, *The New York Times* characterized him as *el abuelito*, "one of the grandfathers of the Chicano literary renaissance," and one of the most "vivid poets of the Chicano literary revival."[4]

Delgado's vibrancy grew out of his repeated call for revolution. Above all, he believed that his Chicano brothers and sisters had experienced the most extreme of life's injustices, and he wrote to urge them toward peaceful protest. In his poem "La Revolución," Delgado writes of those who:

> inspire revolutions,
> because in their desire to right wrongs there are no illusions,
> it is a real manly christian honest desire
> to put injustices here on earth to temporary fire.

Like the revolutionaries he marched beside and admired, Delgado's poetry seeks to extinguish the myriad injustices he watched Mexican Americans endure. He infuses his writing with the same political perspective he brought to Congressional meetings and union rallies for migrant workers; and it is this impassioned voice that urges Chicanos to look beyond poverty, law-enforcement abuse, political oppression and drug-infested streets.

Because he used his poetry to inspire positive change, he maintained that anyone desiring access to his poetry should be able to find it—and to not only find it, but to read it. And to not only read it, but to own it. Thus, he self-published 14 books of poetry under the rubric of Barrio Books, the first of which, *Chicano: 25 Pieces of a Chicano Mind*, sold for $1.50. Yet, there were always some who were unable to pay. Delgado told Lisa Olken of Rocky Mountain PBS Television about a particular gentleman who approached him following a public poetry reading. The man said, "Ay, amigo, I want to read your book, but I don't have $2.00. Will you accept two food stamps?" Delgado laughingly recalls how he then framed those

---

[3]Ibid.

[4]Romero, Simón. "Lalo Delgado, 73, Vivid Poet of Chicano Literary Revival." *New York Times* 30 Jul 2004, A16.

two food stamps and hung them on the wall in his office—underneath a handwritten sign that read, "Poetry is Food."[5] Certainly he wanted his books to be available to anyone willing to read them. And Barrio Books made that possible.

Delgado's poetry offers a unique blend of harsh criticism and gentle humor, which is a duality that parallels his own hybridized, Chicano-American identity. In "Happy 200th Anniversary," Delgado reminds America that "you are my country by choice and not by chance," yet he remains stalwart in his belief that this land of his choosing is capable of:

> historical sins
> errors, premeditated genocides
> robberies, broken treaties, double talk
> and abuses, oppression, imperialistic deeds
> and attitudes, acts of arrogance, racism.

He recalls his own struggle "to understand an anglo's/colorless mind" in "Metamorphosis," and poignantly depicts the emotions at:

> having felt my gut
> hurt as if full of urine
> when I saw an anglo looking down at me.

It is such experiences—in the golden land of opportunity—that led Delgado to conclude that "my integration and segregation are one and the same."[6] Even his own literary being reflects the sad reality of being, at once, an insider *and* an outsider: for while he remains *el abuelito* to those involved with the Chicano movement, his name is hardly recognized in the dominant white culture. Here we see the effect of the distinct but parallel cultures that exist within the United States; here we see the ways in which Delgado's "integration" and "segregation" necessarily converge.

And fittingly, while Delgado uses his own hybridity to tell of the need for visibility, justice and equality, the English-language typewriter upon which he composes his poems does nothing but help erase the very Spanish voice he seeks to validate. Delgado began his literary career at age twelve,

---

[5]Delgado, Abelardo. Interview with Lisa Olken of Rocky Mountain PBS Television. "La Raza de Colorado." Rocky Mountain PBS Television, June 2005.
[6]Ibid.

although the initial reception to his work was harsh and censuring. When he handed his sixth-grade teacher his first written poem, she refused to read it, telling him that the rudimentaries of English—namely spelling and proper punctuation—must come before one can write poetry. Undeterred, the young Delgado eventually found himself a job at the local bowling alley, and used his first paycheck to purchase an Underwood typewriter. In the introduction to his work *Living Life on His Own Terms*, Delgado thoughtfully considers the years he spent with that Underwood:

> Time has caught up with me and I see the golden years engulf me
> and it makes me very sad that I am not the fifteen-year-old boy in
> South El Paso, the first one in the barrio to buy an Underwood typewriter,
> *en abonos*, to type my first poems and cuentos.

This machine enabled Delgado to both write poetry and to learn the intricate and underlying structures of the English language. He would type his verses on any material available to a poor child living in the projects. Indeed, Delgado would later choose to publish his poems with the letterhead upon which they were first written superimposed upon the final printed page. Upon finishing his project, Delgado would painstakingly read through his completed draft, handwriting the appropriate diacritical marks and accents, distinguishing the demonstrative pronouns from the demonstrative adjectives, and inverting the necessary punctuation marks.

Despite the tedium involved in having to make visible his own Spanish language, Delgado continued to write his poetry in a blend of Spanish and English, believing that he could not accurately depict his Mexican roots by writing only in English. He contends that "culture is siphoned through language,"[7] and that if one loses his language, he also loses his culture. His words stress his belief that language can be a useful political tool for resisting oppressive power. In "The Chicano Manifesto," he writes:

> we want to let america know that she
> belongs to us as much as we belong in turn to her
> by now we have learned to talk
> and want to be in good speaking terms
> with all that is america.

[7] Ibid.

And because he has "learned to talk," Delgado also uses his language to reject traditionally derogatory English terms, such as "illegal alien." In "The I.A.," one can see the ways in which language is used as a means of manipulation and control on the part of ruling entities. Here, Delgado asks "the honorable chairman" of a Congressional proceeding to yield "the floor to a Chicano for a minute." He then asks,

> why, what be more unamerican than to have the highest rate of unemployment and play deaf and blind to these "illegal aliens"?

Speaking with Olken, he elaborates on his usage of this term:

> We part company with the term "illegal alien." "Undocumented worker" is our preferred term; for, "illegal" implies that you broke a law. But you break a law to do something more meaningful, which is to subside, to live. It's not a crime to try to live . . . Anything is bad when you use it with the [intent of] being derogatory.[8]

In this way, "The I.A." offers a glimpse of what the embrace of racism might look like if allowed to proceed without restraint:

> occupy mexico. send gavachos to look for work in mexico.
> declare all i.a.s. a communist threat.
> make it all an international harvest game.
> marry them off to every available u.s. dame—

What these examples demonstrate is that Delgado had a keen awareness of the ways in which language can be manipulated or redefined to deny individuals equal rights, and he feared the lasting effects that the integration and continual usage of terms like "illegal alien" would have on undocumented populations. Delgado sensed that power is maintained through language, and thus, in an attempt to subvert the dominant structures at work in the United States, he refused to title this poem with the "derogatory" term he explains in detail above. Rather, he chooses as its title "The I.A" —an acronym for "illegal alien"—to demonstrate that he will in no way dignify the latter usage by giving it any critical weight.

---

[8]Ibid.

Delgado's poetry primarily reflects a deep concern regarding the cultural forces that privilege English over Spanish ("we who speak [two languages] sometimes become victims of the American way of life"), white skin over brown. His poetry speaks of the hegemonic processes at work in the United States and laments that second-generation Chicanos resolve to identify most with white, American culture rather than with their Mexican roots. According to Delgado, "it [assimilation] goes beyond appearance; the way you think is Anglo, and this is because we are indoctrinated by the cultural forces that surround us . . . We are under the influence of the educational system and the media." In his lifetime, Delgado saw this process with his own children and grandchildren. He tells Olken:

> Look what happened to my eight kids. I sent them all to school, and the first thing they did was lose their name: Ana became Anne, Alicia became Alice, Arturo became Art, Alfredo became Freddie, Angélica became Angie, Amelia became Mellie and [Andrea became Andie]. Today we know them that way . . . We can try to hang on to our culture, but with time you will become an Anglo *with* brown skin (emphasis added).[9]

In this telling statement, Delgado's use of the word "with" seems to articulate his greatest concern. For, while he is aware that cultural assimilation is, on some level, possible for the Chicano, he is quick to take his discussion back to the body, back to skin color, back to the "Anglo *with* brown skin." Here, we are back to brownness. And this is where, according to Delgado, the Chicano's complete cultural assimilation is doomed to failure. When questioned as to whether it is difficult to exist in a world where one must struggle to either assimilate or to keep one's own culture, Delgado remarks,

> You are talking to a man who stopped fighting this battle long ago . . . There's no way that I can assimilate because every morning I look in the mirror and I see a . . . Mexican face staring back at me. There's no way that I'm going to be a blonde, blue-eyed Anglo . . . Because of our skin, our desire to assimilate is stopped.[10]

---

[9]Ibid.
[10]Ibid.

Here, Delgado is aware that he simultaneously identifies with—and is alienated from and rejected by—the idealized aspects of dominant white culture; as Homi Bhabha puts it, "not quite/not white."[11] Delgado's writing reflects this reality, speaking to the hearts of Mexican Americans who can see, mapped onto the pages of his poetry, their own struggle for acceptance, for assimilation, in America's racially bifurcated society. Much like Gloria Anzaldúa's new *mestiza consciousness*, Delgado surmises that the Mexican-American subjectivity develops in response to class, gender, religion, region and, above all, race and ethnicity differences. His poetry depicts the vast chasm that exists for Chicanas/Chicanos between physical appearance and the cultural processes that determine the way one thinks. According to Delgado, the former is Mexican; the latter is Anglo.

It is also clear that Delgado writes much as he speaks—with the voice of one manipulating an imported tongue, a borrowed language. Yet, as he acknowledges in "De Corpus a San Antonio," this is a tongue that he has worked to make his own: "what good is my poetic license," he asks, "if i never get to use it?" He goes on,

> because english is my second language
> the endings of english words
> keep throwing me off . . . way off.
> i rhyme love with job
> and orange would rhyme with change or ranch
> or even range.
> they all sound the same to my chicano ear.

Indeed, even the first line of the first poem in Delgado's first published collection shows the subtleties of this dance. In "La Raza," Delgado begins his literary career by writing:

> no longer content with merely shouting *vivas*
> or wearing bright sarape and big sombrero,
> we are coming in if the world will receive us.

---

[11]Bhabha, Homi. "Of Mimicry and Man: The Ambivalence of Colonial Discourse." *Oct* 28 (Spring 1984) 132.

In this line, he identifies the Mexican American's utter refusal to be silent in the face of language barriers and cultural limitations. Or, to quote from Anzaldúa's *Borderlands/La Frontera*, "until I am free to write bilingually [...] while I still have to speak English or Spanish when I would rather speak Spanglish, and as I long as I have to accommodate the English speakers rather than having them accommodate me, my tongue will be illegitimate."[12]

In poems like "Temporary Labor Camp Blues," Delgado writes of the injustices that continue when those affected are not given the opportunity to speak:

> to hear growers through their organization
> representatives sing,
> oops, i mean testify before osha[13], without guitar or violin,
> the sadness of their song brings sudden tears.

According to the poetic voice Delgado gives these representatives, the conditions in the field are adequate:

> the flies are adequate.
> the non-existent toilets are adequate.
> the lack of privacy is adequate.
> but who defines "adequate"?
> where, pray tell, are the affected parties?
> they are in the fields, working, of course.

What we see, in particular, is that it is the plight of the farmworker that moved Delgado's heart. In "The Poor Now Have a Voice," he speaks on behalf of the "skinny malnutritioned bunch" who "migrate in the summers to pick crops of sorts." Much like the seasonal travels of those to whom he dedicates much of his poetry—and his entire professional career—a great deal of his writing is also filled with movement, travel and land.

---

[12]Anzaldúa, Gloria. *Borderlands/La Frontera*. San Francisco: Aunt Lute Books, 1999. 81.

[13]The Occupational Safety and Health Administration (OSHA) is a federal agency of the US government responsible for enforcing safety regulations and protecting the health of America's workers. Delgado testified before OSHA many times in an attempt to pass federal legislation that would improve the standards and working conditions for migrant workers.

In "La Tierra," Delgado composes a work to show the "unison" between Chicanos and the land; he articulates the ways in which the very essence of the Chicano body is something claimed by the land:

a chicano's skin is adobe vented,
his wrinkles are *surcos* that time itself planted,
the mud that in his veins passionately boils,
and his soul something that *la tierra* invented.

Perhaps, then, it is the yearnings of Delgado's soul, created by "la tierra," that usher his movements from place to place. Many of his poems, such as "From Los to Reno," "From Garden City to Hays," "De Corpus a San Antonio" and "De Frisco a Boise," depict his travels, and are titled not according to the cities from which he will either be departing or arriving, but rather within the "from," the "to," the "a," the nebulous place that exists in the movement between destinations.

Delgado wrote "Snow in Albuquerque" while sitting in an airport terminal ("Snow in Albuquerque this late in March caused a bit of pandemonium at the airport"). He opens "Three Margaritas Later" by describing an airport scene:

i already went through the weapon check
at concourse d but my head must be back
at the bar
where mario and i shared three drinks.

And "Friday 12-16-77" begins with the line: "from one airplane to another. I am now on my way to El Paso." This continual travel proved important for Delgado's work, as it led to his belief that multicultural societies would eventually be instrumental in combating racially and culturally motivated oppression.

In this way, Delgado's poetry aligns with the claims James Clifford advances in "Traveling Cultures." Clifford argues that travel is a useful metaphor to describe the borderland, the place of inbetweeness that exists when one is able to view the world outside of a Eurocentric perspective. According to Clifford, the theorist—like the traveler—eventually recognizes that mobility and fluidity express the vision of culture far better than fixed notions of culture as essence. We can thus read the movement in Delgado's poetry as a familiar metaphor for travel, for home and displacement, for borders and crossings, for multiculturalism and change. In Clifford's words, "travel, in this view, denotes a range of material spatial practices that produce knowledge, stories, traditions, music, books, diaries and other cultural expressions" that can be used to disrupt monolithic representations.[14] Certainly poems like "The I. A." speak to this desired multiculturalism, as Delgado provides a solution to many of the problems plaguing America: "open up the borders," he boldly recommends. Here Delgado is working to destabilize fixed notions of culture, with the ultimate goal of dismantling the supposed superiority of the culture of the West. "To theorize, one leaves home," Clifford writes.[15] And, as the titles of his poetry evidence, Lalo Delgado was rarely at home.

It is only in the stillness of "al desierto" that Delgado registers the motion that punctuates his poetry, indeed his life. Speaking of the "silencio" around him, he writes in "Espinas":

> all this was so strange
> to one who is usually surrounded
> in busy airports
> by many many people
> like *espinas*.

This frenzied pace is ultimately appropriate, however, because movement —more specifically the "vast movement for total change," as he puts it in "Requiem for An Ex CAP Director"—is what Delgado spent his entire life championing.

It is arguably this continued need for change that makes a collection like this so necessary. And yet, Delgado himself was painfully aware of the risks of any academic "representation." In "The Chicano Manifesto," he writes:

> you see, you can afford to sit in libraries
> and visit mexico and in a way
> learn to understand us much better than we do ourselves
> but understanding a thing
> and comprehending a thing are two different matters. . . .

---

[14]Clifford, James. "Notes on Travel and Theory." *Inscriptions* 5 (1989), 108.
[15]Ibid, 177

While I do not pretend to "comprehend" the experiences embedded in Delgado's work, I do know that in the years I have spent with his handwritten material on my cluttered desk—and during the evenings I enjoyed in his family home, surrounded by *un ambiente muy acogedor de sus hijos y nietos*—I could not help but "understand." I found myself moved by the sensitivity and humanity of his portrayals, and I knew that his work should again become available to those desiring to access and to *understand* the origins of Chicano literature.

Thus, I first approached this project by wondering whether this collection would do something that Delgado was, himself, unable to do. The answer was no: certainly he had already published, circulated and collected his own work. That work, however, is no longer available to readers.[16] Eventually I questioned whether a project such as this assumes that I—a white, female academic—can speak for a man whose very agenda the white majority culture refused to acknowledge. It was in the midst of this paradox that I found a subtle reconciliation, a quiet urge, propelling me forward. Not only had this project originated because the Delgado family invited and encouraged me to pursue it, but, indeed, Delgado's work showed me that, in some way, all writing seeks to represent other positions in addition to the author's own. Delgado's poetry evokes the voices of racist politicians, white presidents of the United States, Aztec warriors, Mayan goddesses, deceased family members, unborn children, the list could go on. The point, here, is that, as a writer, Delgado recognized the inevitability that someday someone would seek to represent the Chicano voice. As a consequence, he articulates very clearly in "The Chicano Manifesto" the way that that person should proceed:

> deal with us as you openly claim you can,
> justly . . . with love . . . with dignity.

It is my hope that this collection has done just that.

---

[16]For this reason, I have chosen, for this collection, the five volumes (from the fourteen published by Barrio Books) most frequently cited by scholars and used in course syllabi. It should be noted that, aside from the individual works that Delgado self-published, there exists a vast collection of unpublished material at library archives throughout the United States. While the largest, unpublished collection of work still remains with the Delgado family, the Benson Latin American Collection at the University of Texas at Austin and the archives at Metropolitan State College, the University of Colorado at Boulder and the University of Arizona also have collections of Delgado's work.

CHICANO: 25 pieces of a chicano mind (1969)

*dedicated to
the mexican-american migrant*

La Raza

no longer content with mearly shouting *vivas*
or wearing bright sarape and big sombrero,
we are coming in if the world will receive us
as humans and not as pinto bean amoebas.

raza evolving, ever stronger, ever one,
filling the Spaniard olive merging shadow
and kneeling with the indian worshipping the sun
and fighting revolutions with a rusty gun.

we, raced or razed mestizos shouldering conquest
and enduring the harsh whip upon our *cuero*
having had our sacred origin need no quest
to find identity or set our souls at rest.

though *méjico* is *la madre patria* we go
the world over seeking only greener meadow;
poetic, sentimental, proud, copper ego
serving as an emblem to a dream's *testigo*.

identified by a last name or a language
full of *picardía*, *raza* placed *primero*,
raza placed to serve as paste to close the wedge
between the human and the divinely alleged.

raza which fortunately includes the many
who in the midst of poverty build a grotto;
unfortunately, *vendidos* for a penny,
agringados who think macho is uncanny.

the national, green carder, U.S. citizen,
the *pocho*, the *manito* and the *bracero*,
the Mex-Tex, what's the difference? *olvídensen*,
it's the milk, *raza*, that an indian's *chichi* sent.

La Huelga

wash well your throat with *tequila*
so that your voice comes out *tranquila*
and then softly whisper . . . *huelga* . . .
or . . . shout *huelga* with anger
as if someone had killed your parents,
someone has . . .
get off your comfortable ass
and join the choir,
sing to your lung's capacity
huelga . . . *huelga* . . . *huelga*.

say *huelga* with love
for the unborn *chicanitos*,
put the salt of your tears into it.
don't be one more *estúpido*
thinking *huelga* only means strike,
shout it any way you like
say *huelga* over and over
like an ave maría.
huelga with joy
for today the sixteenth of September
and July the fourth have gone to bed together.
huelga with despair
for it is the last word
that chicano will utter
before he turns himself to boiling butter.

La Tierra

la tierra is *la raza*'s kissing cousin,
she's the patient mother who will listen
to the sun-baked lament of the one who toils,
she's playmate to the growing dozen.

she's the sweetheart of young chicano dreamers
decorating those dreams with live green streamers,
she's the woman with the perfumed sexy soils,
her somber existence through yonder glimmers.

she is the banner of the revolution
and wide battlefield and source of its solution,
nourishment of men or mirror of turmoils,
womb of all that starts, tomb of all conclusion.

méjico got some of you back . . . how dismal,
new mexicans reclaim you . . . odds abysmal
and texans wash their hands with your spat-out oils,
while californians sing from your gold hymnal.

men love you, hate you, regulate you,
they sell you, trade you and speculate you,
they build, they plant, they mine and from your despoils
bring life . . . comfort, riches and glamour anew.

while the arabs and jews over you dispute
the price of your foot an anglo will compute,
but only the soul of one, like a snake recoils,
soul chicano which unison it can't repute.

look . . . a chicano's skin is adobe vented,
his wrinkles are *surcos* that time itself planted,
the mud that in his veins passionately boils,
and his soul something that *la tierra* invented.

El Macho

how does your own culture judge you a *macho*?
how soon do you stop being a *muchacho*?
why do you wear as heart a ripe *pistachio*
and why does it pump contrasts instead of blood?

I'm the measure by which my culture judges,
I am a man at twelve needing no crutches,
I wear a heart that has no room for grudges,
my whole being is a paradox of mud.

tell, why does an *hembra* find you attractive?
does a man think your friendship is protective?
why does suffering find you none receptive
and why is your anger like a human flood?

women find my love brutal yet so gentle,
'cause a man knows my friendship will all mantle,
suffering and I grew in the same ventral,
my anger cries justice as if I were God.

tell me, *macho*, why does your bronze forehead swell
as if in it was housed heaven or hell?
with your gaze alone an enemy you fell,
are, are you that good, you literal brown stud?

the Indian pride I house in me is the earth
which gives us food and life its true worth,
my dark eyes can also wake the dead with myrth,
not a stud but stallion choosing my own cud.

why must your word be always final and curt
and must you, mexican masochist, hunt hurt?
will you even compromise 'til death from birth?
will you let me use your brown divining rod?

my word is a contract that my handshake signs,
pain is my thing, it's with it that my soul refines,
compromising is machismo's parting lines,
you can't use my rod, I use it when I nod.
my sentiments are raw, my tears come easy,
my spanish soul is always in a tizzy,
I think it's she and not my skin that's greasy,
hombre cabal is *macho* not a male bud.

La Hembra

mujer mexicana, queen playing submissive,
you alone can disarm a macho with your charms,
the only strong chains he knows are your loving arms,
your cinnamon breasts are two fire alarms.

the four stages of your life are all inclusive
you are the little girl with two long black *trenzas*,
taking with your almond eyes the world's census,
shaping a body which will be all sensuous.

nature was without reserve quite permissive
in granting a *señorita* such perfection
combining grace and dare in her every action,
bet when she falls in love it is a free election.

when her flower opens it's a time exclusive
for there is no fire equal her kiss or sweetness,
a way to make her man crave for her nearness
is to make him of her love a living witness.

no woman will cling to youth, the fast illusive,
with such tenacious abandon as she does,
carrying a *niño* in her womb is the crux
of all femininity that forever was.

her joy, her love, her endurance, is impressive
but the way she suffers almost without a tear
makes the *hembra chicana* divinely appear,
makes her life fully mysterious and yet so clear.

your critics whisper your life is dull, reclusive,
deep down they envy your serene security,
you can give and take all with such maturity,
you can change pain to joy and lust to purity.

La Causa

what moves you, chicano, to stop being polite?
nice chicano could be patted on the head and wouldn't bite
and now, how dare you tell your boss, "go fly a kite?"
    es la causa, hermana, which has made me a new man.

what is this *causa* which disturbs your steady hand,
could it be an inherited love of land
or the indian impudence called pride that I can't understand?
    this cause, *hermano,* is charcoaled abuse ready to burn.

what nonsense this brown power that you claim,
what stupid demands erupt from wills untamed,
what of your poetic submissiveness that brought you fame?
    es la causa, hermano, which leaves no one untouched.

delano awaits the verdict of the nation,
del río and justice dance in wild anticipation,
el paso and *la causa* will be good for the duration
    es la causa, hermano, raping apathy with flair.

san antonio cannot sleep another night,
los angeles cannot forfeit another fight,
denver cannot hide from us its burning light,
    es la causa, hermano, don't let our heroes feel betrayed.

albuquerque trembles with the blast of sacrifice
y todo el valle carries life at a cheap price,
los barrios y los campos become a symphony of cries,
    es la causa de la raza an anthill upon your chest.

la causa for all those blindly involved who do not know
is the planting of *mañanas* which will grow
permitting the faceless chicanos of that day to go
    like eagles, as high as they can, as high as they want to.

El 16 de Septiembre

independence is a thing that's old
and man values it much more than gold.
mexico wanted to rid *indios* of their yoke
and its *valientes* and guns together spoke.

three centuries of domination
and abuse call for termination,
the rape and the abuse, the thievery and the lie
got to where it was much better to die.

the mestizo jacinto camek,
pipila with a rock on his back,
costilla, morelos, domínguez, allende,
and aldama . . . *revolución* . . . *prende*!

when the right time came it beat the plan,
justice will not a minute wait . . . it can't
and so *vivas* on the sixteenth of september
began a change we will long remember.

morelos went south, virgin in front,
guns and machetes ending much want,
liberation was the word . . . out the *gachupín*
all chicanos were out to die or win.

yet today in nineteen sixty nine
causes for revolting are now mine . . .
denver . . . on denver, chicanos march together
aztlán, all your youth is hard as leather.

El Inmigrante

golondrinas cortando betabel,
americanos de papel,
este méxico-americano
o nomás mejicano
que migra con to' y familia
a los campos de colorado,
illinois, califa y michigan
se me hace que no es más que puro gitano.
salmones en el desaije
con un ojo a las colonias
a las cuales muy pronto volverán,
no les voy
a decir por qué lo hacen
porque la verdad ni ellos saben,
quizá el cariño a la tierra
mamado de una chichi prieta,
quizá el corazón libre
que dicta la jornada,
aunque el carro esté muy viejo
y la gasolina cara.
turistas sin un centavo
de vacación en nebraska,
aún alabama
es un descanso de tejas.
bumerangas que la mano de dios
por este mundo tiró,
gente buena,
gente honesta,
gente víctima de su necesidad de migrar,
la lechuga o la justicia es lo que van a sembrar.

Poema

llevas en tu anchos hombros, mexicano,
el peso de una lucha que parece en vano.
el látigo del patrón benévolo cruzó tu espalda,
razgó de la humilde india el español la falda.
robó tu tierra y la labró con tu labor esclava,
con la ignorancia ató la única libertad que te quedaba.
por mucho que quepa en la tinaja un día se llena
y se volvió en grito tu sufrir por mucho tiempo gema.
se volvió fusil el azadón que tu empuñabas,
trincheras sangradas los surcos que con fe sembrabas.
no es nacional sino mundial lo que tú has hecho,
contagia igual el deseo que hinchó tu negro pecho.
no fue un diez y seis de septiembre el día
para que tocara la trompeta su libre melodía.
fue el día que un dios crio al hombre
y le otorgó de libre conquistador no conquistado su nombre.
la revolución cambia hoy en día de forma
pero la cuestión social aún carece de reforma.
la carrillera aquella de vaqueta corriente
es hoy la palabra que nace y brota de una triste frente.
se trata aún de unirse codo con codo
y hoy como ayer se gana . . . o se pierde todo.

Cactus Fruit

a little *jacal* up in washington for us, we are proud,
we the mexican-american youth thank our president out loud
but a *jacal* built with pride no politics can break
and a new administration will only more adobes bake.
the *nopal* is old but we are the fruit, the youth,
the future is our *montoncito* too, we are not mute,
we are not deaf, nor dumb, we are maya, we are alert,
we are *la raza* experimenting a new birth.
God himself made his *morena* mother create
us mestizos, us chicanos, 1531 was the date,
and her *cobija* reached but well the U.S. west;
spaniards, indians, mexicans, americans and none the best.
our *abuelos* toiled the land and grabbed the rifle
our machismo will not let us now settle for a trifle,
whoever our leaders are we not only follow and trust
but with us the full commitment of the spirit is a must.
our nation must stop biting its tongue calling us sons
for when it comes top time for a showdown we are the ones
who little hesitate to fight, to sacrifice and die
but we too like to walk in dignity looking at the sky.
basta is a *grito* we respect and know but well
and we in choir shout it now to the five corners of hell,
we have no more generations for anyone to waste,
we've eaten crumbs but we have developed a new taste.
The time to study us like foreign wild animals is gone,
we welcome help but resent aid that's followed by a stone,
we no longer wish *la raza*'s name be called in vain,
we are maya, we are the cactus fruit soaking up the rain.
thorny but sweet like *tunas mejicanas* we will meet
anyone, anytime, any place like *hombres* in complete,
but we will not allow any doubletalk at all
for our dark eyes retain or give our very soul.

El Compadre

I dono why, *compadre,* but this dance
looks like it is going to end *como las otras*
with a hell of a brawl *y muchos chingazos* . . .
they've been givin' me the dirty *ojo* . . .
vale más irnos, compadre . . .
you 'no, *compadrito,* it's good you are with me
otherwise I would be more afraid,
they are four tough-looking *batos* . . .
and frankly I am not in the mood
for *cabronazos,*
mire . . . compadre . . . I think . . .
they are coming after us . . .
vámonos, pronto a pelarle de aquí . . . entrust us
to the saint *que le dio en la madre al dragón*
because here they come
and they don't want
no conversation . . . *ay* . . .
ya me aterrizaron el primero . . . compadre,
pase una manita,
where are you? . . . don't leave me,
they'll kill me . . .
I am sorry, *compadre*
pero los jodazos duelen
y de que le den a los dos . . . pues . . .

A César Chávez

tu sueño es contagioso, hermano,
ya toda la nación sufre tu fiebre justiciera
se ha originado en el pueblo de delano
y corre el germen atacando conciencias por doquiera.

te oímos en ft. lupton por la boca de herrera
y el pao tenía a pablo que hablé de ti con ojos aluzados,
tu mensaje es uno que va muy de carrera,
levantando las frentes de pizcadores empinados.

tony y dolores son dos vocinas de confianza,
tanto creen en lo que por nosotros buscas
que cuando hablan de ti se convierte su voz en alabanza
y tu sueño bello hace que ante todos te trasluzcas.

oye, césar, la subida cuesta arriba ha sido dura
oye, chávez, no te canses que mis hijos crecen ya,
descansa un poco que ya cogió fuego la llanura
y el enemigo en vez de enfrentarse se nos va.

california ya es bajada, tejas se cairá,
colorado espera sólo un grito, Arizona ya está lista,
nuevo méjico aunque pequeño muy alto saltará
y luego michigan y utah, no esperan que nada las resista.

mira, viejo, que la juventud chicana ansía,
mira a la hembra, mujer, madre y hermana,
miran a tu servicio mil mentes como la mente mía . . .
¿oyes sonar sonora la campana? ¿oyes cantar a la guadalupana . . .

El Barrio

I am that piece of land "la ciudad" is trying to hide,
I house "gente" to whom the American Dream has lied,
in my corners stand the youth "morena" with no future,
in my "callejón" walls' graffiti find their nomenclature.
my aroma of hunger brings "muerte" to the table,
Monday's wash on the "tendederos" tells a torn fable
as a "chisme" dripping away from old women's parched
mouths,
I act as stereo amplifying clearly "dolor" shouts.
my "calles" shudder littered with the weight of many needs,
my "ambiente" is constant S O S so that no one heeds.
I am the alma mater of lost "almas" and bodies,
"yo soy" the unkept laboratory where man studies,
erupting like a volcano "con un" upset stomach
"escupo" the sick, the delinquent, I am a hammock
to the "prostituta," a cemetery to ambition,
a corner to "talento," no exit just admission.
"yo soy el barrio," the slum, the ghetto, progress' sore
thumb,
my zombies live "por hoy" and their children have grown
     pain numb,
collectively I am a spirit "que es" explosive,
"yo fabrico" defeat of a quality that's plausive,
conservatively, comfortably "soy casa" of all
who suffer, thirst and hunger, "formando" precious rubble,
I am "humano," my skin absorbs with ease diseases,
through the marrow of my weak "huesos" a rat releases,
playful "cucarachas" and dancing lice, festive pieces
as the barrio readies for "la venida" of Jesus.

El Río Grande

jorobado, arrugado, seco, como viejo mal cuidado
va mi río grande ya menos apurado
con el zoquete del tiempo manchado,
por dos países maltratado y decorado.

si en vez de crujir tus aguas platicaran
que de hazañas no nos contaran
y si tus granos de arena miraran
cuánta mentira con su mirar nos desataran.

has visto sufrir al mejicano
cambiar su sudor por tus aguas mano a mano,
tú le has dado a la lechuga el chile como hermano
y al tomate le cambiaste en algo humano.

en ancas de una mula cuando niño te crucé,
miras tú el contrabando que el de la aduana no ve,
sirves de espejo a la esperanza que se fue
y vives esperando la lluvia que una nube negra dé.

río grande, polvo de tejas, ramas, de nuevo méjico las ramas,
duermes bajo la luz de luciérnagas y la música de ranas,
para los enamorados tus orillas son mil camas
y de un amarillento carrizo son tus canas.

tu fama nacional es como una noche oscura
y tus aguas tiñen de una sangre insegura,
eres tú la puerta más cruel y la más dura.
separas al hombre y haces de su ambición basura.

leí que se ahogó un mejicano que te quizo cruzar
venía a los estados unidos y su muerte fue a encontrar,
un día tus fuerzas como las fronteras se van a acabar . . .
háblame pronto, río grande, que el tiempo te va a matar.

Narciso

how my honesty is disarming
is even to me quite alarming
but the other day
I met a fellow
who disarmed me.
he wanted to look into your eyes
(the cold-blooded bastard)
and not remove his wounding look
until you answered him
with a simple yes or no,
he speaks of his life
as . . . my life which will be short . . .
young fellow too,
but I guess
in the newly initiated
business of being honest
one must be honest
even with oneself.
he is *número tres*
in my collection
of beautiful people,
his name is narciso . . .
I do hope the times
do not contaminate him
and he continues to stare down injustices.
but even more
that he learns to love humanity
and even those who cause calamity.

El Chisme

with more accuracy than an ol' time *pistolero*
and with the advantage of arriving there *primero*
el chisme soap suds clean, the chicano's *noticiero*
can penetrate solid steel *con más ganas* reach an ear.

la vecina's zippered lip can, gentle, non offensive, appear
but even chet and david lack the details that she has
if she didn't see it happen *se imagina lo que es,*
she's not happy with the facts 'til she turns them *al revés.*

the network is so well organized that it now predicts
with much precision where the gallup polls will not come near
what the *chisme* gets going not the devil contradicts
and church cannons look puny against the *chisme's* edicts.

what baffles even the most of modern computations
is how one *chisme* ruins a million reputations
and another broadcasting from the same mouth makes you fear
just proof that many tongues need immediate amputations.

The Majic Valley

san juan, I walked your streets at noon,
weslaco, I found my street too soon,
mission, pharr, edinburg, mcallen,
donna and I don't know all the others
I drove through
last Thursday morn at two,
but I saw your humid *palmeras*
and heard the quimeras
of chicanos who love you,
el valle, sur tejas,
they are busy, *pobrecitos,*
arguing with machines
which took their jobs away,
with the rude *troqueros*
who have lost their humanity
in one of those deals they make,
yes, san juan, I ate
huevos rancheros
y tortillas de maíz,
I taped a couple of poems
for one of your radio stations
and I understood
why they call you magic;
the magic they speak of
is the love
chicanos have for you when they should hate
the misery you bring them,
with your laws of cold unconcern,
with the love you don't return.

La Revolución

some dream of revolutions
after all they are also one of the solutions
but in their dream they neglect to take into account
that real characters participate in them.
some fight relevant revolutions
they mean to bring with bullets needed absolutions
and like players of that one dream they act their parts
and for a minute in their fight they too dream.
some betray revolutions,
they start out endorcing with hearty allocutions
the evident need for reform but to them
the bodies of revolutionaries are merely stepping stones.
some inspire revolutions,
because in their desire to right wrongs there are no illusions,
it is a real manly christian honest desire
to put injustices here on earth to temporary fire.

mexico became an early model
of that dream, that fight, that betrayal, that inspiration
but not in the words of *hombres ilustres*
or even in the words of *generales valientes*
can the wisdom or sense of *la revolución* be found
but in the thick lips of a prospective *soldado razo*
about to join *las tropas* at a crossroad.

where are you going? why are you fighting?
¿cuál es la causa?
who is the enemy?
and after hearing only silence for an answer
to his painful questions
he gives a big *grito* . . .
wait . . . wait for me *yo voy con ustedes* . . .
but the *moreno capitán* does not accept
his enthusiasm

and looking into his *dos carbones* of a pair of eyes
asks . . . why do you want to come with us?
'cause your *revolución* cannot be as bad as the life I'm living
ven, pues, you're fiber with which the change sarape we
      are weaving.

Mamá Lupe

you labored in pain at tepeyac hill
to give soul birth to a race of strong will,
your apparitions spoke the indian tongue,
your very words were in that language sung.

lupe, mother of the *taparabos*,
follows her child wherever her child goes,
lupe, mother of *putas* and thieves,
like sunshine and rain falls the love she gives.

root of God and of mestizos as well
like a mother as far as we can tell
she asks nothing of her children and gives all,
she sits in heaven waiting for his call.

miracle of chemistry and numbers,
housed your picture now in golden chambers,
to you kneeling *indios* still proudly crawl
and when they kiss the ground stand most tall.

lupe in my wallet and on the wall
mamá lupe, estrellas in her shawl
morena dulce, don't do what I do
and forget me like I've forgotten you.

La Guadalupana

december twelve fifteen thirty-one *la raza* was born
on mount tepeyac *una bella india* from heaven
standing on the moon, covering *el sol*, dressed with the stars
performed a mathematical miracle baptizing
indios by the millions over night for her other son.
a hanging, visible, touchable *arte en costal*
drawn with twelve winter roses soaked in the bold blood
    of God,
my flesh mother bears your name with pride, sometimes
    with scorn,
guadalupe, take charge of the third one of my seven,
guadalupe, mother of *putas* who hang around bars,
also of taxi drivers cherry hill advertising,
mother of the revolution's still working rusty gun,
mamá de los ojos negros, de pensamiento fatal
you alone say . . . am I not here . . . when we overshoot
    our wad.

El 26 de Agosto

tiembla ciudad del paso
que hoy hablan tus chicanos
tiembla nación de América
que ya se llaman hermanos.
miran ellos con un herido coraje
y buscan con sus miradas
un hombre como ellos que no se raje.
suena agudo el grito verde
que proclama raza y causa
y la juventud chicano alega
que ya no hay tiempo pa' pausa.
vienen desde muy lejos
porque ya se acude luego
al grito de otro chicano
y hoy es desafío lo que antes era su ruego.
el segundo barrio y juárez
se les hinchan adobes y ladrillos
de ver morenos parados y muy derechos
y ver juntos a los caudillos.
alemán vino de michigan,
compeán desde san antonio,
el corky voló de denver,
orendain desde san juan, o del demonio,
unos batos de califa,
y uno desde nueva york
y todos fueron bien recibidos
por los líderes del paso . . .
el pipis, el melo, el chacha y el geras
junto con tony moreno
van a enseñarle a los gringos lo que es
            ser de deveras . . .

Un Telegrama

ora narciso . . . ya se nos hizo,
tijerina traí carabina,
chávez ya traí las llaves,
cha cha afila el hacha,
valenzuela ya va que vuela,
ora ramírez . . . no te me estires,
ora pipis pa' que desquites,
de león traí buen cañón,
ora gordo . . . no te hagas sordo,
orendain a ver que train,
ora, tú, lalo dales un palo,
tú, compeán que se nos van,
tafolla ya está que atolla,
delgado . . . por aquel lalo,
elizondo . . . ya está en lo hondo,
quintanilla ya formó orilla,
sánchez pa' que te enganches,
cantú, encomiendate a belcebú,
lópez dales que te los topes,
también tú, hernández, no le hace dónde andes,
tú, ruiz por la matriz,
mientras que esmeralda cuida la espalda,
atencio, guarda silencio,
valdez no te me des,
chaca con la matraca,
herrera, échalos en carrera,
memo, a darles que ya me quemo,
nino viene con el vecino,
aguilar, guarda el lugar,
moreno, échales trueno,
pallanez, no te desganes,
tú, orona, por la pelona,
gonzales, enseña tú lo que vales,
ávila, ponte más águila

rivera, no se te olivde la carrillera . . .
ojeda, fíjate a ver quién queda . . .
pérez, no desesperes

este telegrama fue firmado por el presidente de los
estados unidos
este día de nuestro snowman _____.

Stupid America

stupid america, see that chicano
with a big knife
in his steady hand
he doesn't want to knife you
he wants to sit down on a bench
and carve christ figures
but you won't let him.
stupid america, hear that chicano
shouting curses on the street
he is a poet
without paper and pencil
and since he cannot write
he will explode.
stupid america, remember that chicanito
flunking math and english
he is the picasso
of your western states
but he will die
with one thousand masterpieces
hanging only from his mind.

El Vendido

my son is a sellout
he just became a boy scout.
I would like to entertain
the notion of sellouts
or *vendidos* as we say
a la chicano.
josé lópez has been working
as a janitor for the last twelve years
today he got a two dollar raise
and today also he has been accused
by the barrio of being a *vendido,*
josé is thinking very seriously
of refusing the raise
to preserve his barrio image.
if a man is not made
to deviate from his goal
all his actions,
whatever they may be,
disqualify him as a sellout.
a man sells out
the minute he compromises
with a different goal
and needs not the criticism
of his chicano brothers
for he (the funny thing about selling out)
pays for himself.
finally no chicano can sell himself
for you see, he is too dumb,
he has not arrived at a price
or could it be he is too wise.

The Chicano Manifesto

this is in keeping with my own physical condition
for I am tired—too tired perhaps for this rendition . . .
but *la raza* is also tired
and *la raza* cannot wait
until I rest
she wants her rest also
but there is much catching up to do.
anglos have asked (I think sincerely)
what it is that you chicanos want?
those with power to be,
influencing our lives, have asked . . .
is it understanding?
is it that you want us to tolerate you?
is it admittance?
and when I heard those questions
like remote control my chicano anger took over
and I answered the arrogant questioning . . .
no . . . we do not want any of that
or the question "what do you want" either
you see, you can afford to sit in libraries
and visit mexico and in a way
learn to understand us much better than we do ourselves
but understanding a thing
and comprehending are two different matters . . .
tolerate is a word we use
in reference to *borrachos*,
we do not wish you strain
yourselves with toleration
of our, supposedly, intolerable ways
and . . . yes . . . question of admittance
is a fine one for it puts you inside and us outside
asking like cats and dogs in the rain to be let in.
the nature of your questions
assumes you have something to offer.

but there is one thing I wish
you would do for us,
in all of your dealings with us,
in all your institutions
that affect our lives
deal with us as you openly claim you can,
justly . . . with love . . . with dignity.
correct your own abuses on *la raza*
for your own sake and not for ours
so you can have some peace of mind
for . . . you see . . . we only lack a piece of bread
which comes cheaper according to your own value system
let me tell you what we want,
not from you but from ourselves and for ourselves . . .
we want to let america know that she
belongs to us as much as we belong in turn to her
by now we have learned to talk
and want to be on good speaking terms
with all that is america.
from government we want to become
visible and not merely legislated
and supervised but included
in the design of laws and their implementation.
from education we want the most that it can offer,
a history that tells it like it is,
principals, teachers, counselors, college professors . . .
and all this from chicanos *a la chicana*
and this we are not asking *por favor*
but merely as an overdue payment
and we might even forget the previous score.
from the church we very piously ask
less sermon and more delivery
more priests to preach Christ's merciful justice,
less alms and tokens in the name of charity
and more pinpointment of the screwing going on.
from *los chicanos del barrio y de los campos*
we also have some strong demands

(among ourselves there is much more *confianza*)
we want you to plot a clean escape but very soon,
lose your habit of speaking in low voices
and of walking with *cabezas agachadas*,
you are poor only in material
for your heritage is very rich.
from chicanos with a little
bit of wealth and power *les*
pedimos una mano
but to give *los olvidados*
not a damn thing . . . they are asking
for your hand . . . but only in *amistad*
as brothers that you, even if you don't want to, are.
and finally to the draft board
we have a few words to share with you
no la jodan . . . metan gabachos también . . .
our manifesto I know is general
but we saved the especific for the end
for the chicano migrant is about
to become like your American buffalo . . . extinct . . .
those who claim that was a crime with animals
are now in good position to prevent one with humans
or will the migrants honor come as always . . . posthumous.

Bajo el Sol de Aztlán
(1973)

Snow in Albuquerque

this late in March caused a bit of pandemonium at the air-
port. I saw from the airplane the cold white blanket over
city and plains. Nature's way of whitewashing a city. It
gave me a couple of free hours to enter into the prepara-
tion of choosing some old versos y poemas to read in and
around Phoenix and Tucson in my ten-day reading tour.
This tour will pay for the tortillas and beans which my
wife and eight children as well as I will eat during April
provided food prices stay put or else I may have to do
without the tortillas *y entrarle al puro biro*.

About this place in most of my introductions I'm supposed
to say something profoundly philosophical or philosophi-
cally profound. I will bypass that by merely mentioning
that my daughter, Amelia, gets a penny for every white
hair she gets from my otherwise dark *cabellera*. My *canas*
are a good source of income for her as the other Saturday
she was up to two dollars and eighteen cents when I told
her to stop, I was afraid she would leave me *pelón*. They
say that white hair is a symbol of maturity, respect, worry
and many other such. At forty-one the only symbol I see
is getting old. The *canas* go well with my size 42 *panza*
and my bitter mellow verse. —*Se te pasó el bus*, Lalo, —I
tell myself at nights before going to sleep, meaning my
chances of becoming a great writer or a great anything are
all gone as my energy and creativity decreases in propor-
tion to the hard *topes que me da la vida*.

Last night in my easy chair I sat through the dramatiza-
tion on tv of the Pueblo Incident and got pretty emotional-
ly shook with the program. Things like that and movies
such as "Walking Tall" influence my writing, not to men-
tion the Watergate mess, the Supreme Court's decision on
equal educational opportunities, evidently defined by
them as those with money rightfully having a bit more of

the equal access. A four to five decision affecting four to five million Chicano children, blacks, indians and poor whites.

The price of steak and eggs has made me and my thoughts turn socialist or communist, at least while I'm by the cash register trying to pay for the *carrito de mandado*. The reason being that I could care less what things cost as I go around picking what I feel like eating and not looking at the price per pound. But . . . here's the big "but" . . . what of the *carnales* who don't make a hundred a day consulting, training or reading poems? They do not only have to look but to do without. Such thoughts do much to destroy my appetite and I cannot enjoy the food I can afford at any price.

I can only manage to maintain my optimism, my faith in life, in god, in America by becoming proportionally insane or plotting, when I am not expressing that insanity in poetry, some escape routes or looking for common denominators that would weld us humans divine or us divine humans. Gold at $105.00 an ounce, poetry at 22¢ a line and eggs at 95¢ a dozen (extra large) . . . *pos qué pedo . . . vendo el oro, escribo el verso y me como unos huevos rancheros.*

Aquí

aquí . . . hoy . . . por siempre en adelante . . . nosotros,
bajo el sol de aztlán juramos unos a los otros
apoyo, cariño, respeto, confianza y carnalismo.
vivir esclavos y haber muerto en vida es casi lo mismo.

aquí, con los ojos y a la vez la mente clara
hoy, ante todo el mundo el chicano libre se declara,
y para eso con un fuerte abrazo, aquí
la vida misma tú me prometes . . . te prometo a ti.

aquí, en la cuna de la revolución social chicana
hoy, cinco de mayo, la raza libre y soberana
declaramos con el pecho en llamas el orgullo
que cada chicano por ser chicano tiene como suyo.

aquí, nos hemos decidido . . . no a emprender camino
sino a aumentar el paso y enseñar a todos lo fino
que es ser chicano y lo sagrado de nuestra causa
y les recordamos que ya no es tiempo de pausa.

aquí, sientan absorber, de uno a otro, la fuerza
del espíritu de nuestro movimiento que es inmensa
e invencible . . . poco es lo que queremos,
vivir como hombres libres . . . o mejor moramos.

Why Am I Here?

ey, carnal, why are you here with all your brothers?
why do you raise questions with which no one else both-
ers?
ey, carnal, what was it that you felt as we walked?
why *mañanas* did your *espíritu* kept going on to stalk?

why am i here? *eh . . . qué va . . .* because i belong!
i raise questions 'cause i sense that something's wrong
and as i walked i felt, well . . . *libre* . . . a free man—
more than that, as a chicano, which only another can
        understand.

my spirit seeks noble and worthy fulfillment of my dreams,
a place where no one against another any longer schemes
and where the word "underprivileged" is buried,
yeah, *carnal,* if i'd known earlier i'd have hurried.

i cannot help but know that while i am here
there are others who are yet prisoners of fear
and are content to read of us tomorrow,
for these *carnales* i cannot help but sorrow.

my spirit goes to all the *hermanos* wasted away
but here i am and they are gone and here . . . today
i pledge before all of my *raza* not to rest
until the chicano way of life is proven best.

Erline

i drank words from lips shaped nice
and sip'd the coolness of your green eyes
and lost track very fast
of what those words meant
for there in the crowded
breakfast table of the "red lion"
i savagely had mental
communion and i was
caressing, kissing, sexing
your spirit in spite of your body,
and pancakes and coffee
i breakfasted you
naked on the tablecloth
warming with your body
food for the intimate meals
of lonely souls,
of souls of complete strangers
who knew not one another
just last sunday
but in the timeless world
of eternity where souls do live
reality is only that which you believe.

Museum Piece

collector's item three thousand and nine,
a poor, poor friend of mine,
the last of his kind . . .
you see, it came to be
that in this blessed country of ours
where impossibilities
are not allowed
(we had to use the "not allowed" signs
with space on top)
we decided to end poverty
and got damn serious about it,
first o.e.o. took a crack at it
but it seemed to do the opposite
by multiplying the poor
like their rented duplicating machines
multiplied survey forms,
the whole government threw its weight
behind such noble efforts . . . to no avail,
even the church took action
after combing through
the obscure passages
of the king james (revised) edition
but, alas, they could not either
come up with a solution,
other than giving poverty holy absolution.
it was not until the mafia,
the cosa nostra,
the brotherhood said enough to poverty
that almost overnight poverty ceased
to become only an americana museum piece.

Metamorphosis

my integration consists
(my, how the thought persists)
of having kissed an anglo girl
once, twice, a hundred times.
my integration consists
of having married an anglo girl
(ceremony was in latin, tho)
my integration consists
of having once
fiercely punched an anglo man
once, twice, a hundred times.
my integration consists
of having once tried
to understand an anglo's
colorless mind,
my integration consists
of having felt my gut
hurt as if full of urine
when i saw an anglo looking down at me.
my integration consists
(and here i end all lists)
of having become an anglo
without having died
and without having been born again,
my integration and segregation are one and the same.

Twin Falls

twin falls . . . or is it twin spirits
out of the same desire born?
the desire to be free
>   *el uno, el espíritu de orgullo,*
>   *el otro, el espíritu de amor,*
>   *el uno, una espina. el otro, una flor.*
que a toda es vernos aquí de nuevo,
verda' de dios—two years later, to come
back here and show each other the battle wounds,
to remember the drops of frustration flowing,
salting the *bigotes* of great hombres
>   *y las mejillas de mujeres finas,*
>   *enseñarnos dónde nos hemos*
>   *herido uno al otro,*
>   *dónde el sueño nos mintió,*
>   *dónde nosotros le mentimos al* dream *que teníamos.*
>   *—vamos hoy a apartar derrotas de victorias.*
y pedro y rogelio y beto y lula y celia
y lópez y ligas, benavidez, sánchez y silva,
y reyna y dionicio y julie y héctor y maría,
i swear i have seen all these *carnales y carnalas* before
in some ancient aztec city, weaving aztlán
with their own blood, shading *al sol con su plumaje fino*
or *zapateando coplas en la vieja españa,*
descanzando al fin del surco, buying groceries
en el valle de tejas, en lubbock, *en* crystal, *en* laredo,
dying by the *trincheras en la revolución,*
crossing the río grande, riding in the back of trucks,
and today—*resollamos hondo,*
enterramos las diferencias, las envidias,
el odio y la movida chueca, el insulto
y marchamos juntos siguiendo a la esperanza
en un nuevo día, el camino es aún angosto
pero la libertad siempre se ha pagado al costo.

Oh, Shit

even though the title of this poem isn't romantic
it is a phrase that speaks of love that is authentic,
i find myself
thinking of you more and more,
you are right,
it is unfair
to only taste a food
so appetizing . . . once . . . twice . . .
taste when one wants to devour
such was an episode we can call ours,
 . . . waking up in my arms,
i, feeling your naked body near,
warm, satisfied
and safe,
oh, shit,
right, echo that in loud
musical notes
or sing it like a franciscan chant
or let a choir
do encores on . . .
oh, shit . . . oh, shit . . . oh, shit
and pretty soon
the vulgarity of such a phrase
goes away and it becomes pure and lovely
just like you have often uttered it,
once, while half-kneeling
half-sitting
in the moonlight,
moon, which even now is jealous of my touches
and continues to blush as she watches.

La Secre

this secretary who wears no panties
is a revolutionary aprentice,
she takes dictation
and types stencils
but her contribution
to the movement
ends not there
she also moves
with the movement,
drinking tequila,
shouting *ay . . . ay . . . ay,*
o' i know she's anglo,
anglos no longer just fund
revolutions
and run guns
now they get involved
and at times even refuse
to vacate the front
but getting back to this secretary
with the legs
which could make a nice
guide on a flag
she is really dedicated,
vindicated, abdicated
and come to think of it
for her it will be easy
to become a chicano colonel
by just marrying a chicano
and dying brown her pretty *ano.*

My Unborn Sons (Or Daughters)

flowering words
not yet sure of
their gender
or their meaning
they crowd the shelves
of my unused mind
they rattle now
and then only
to remind
themselves and i
that they exist
ready to describe
some new emotions,
some distant days,
some smiling faces . . . .
for now, they sleep
for i have trivia to keep.

Laloisms

there are many who are not afraid
to shout openly—*viva la causa*
but how many are willing
to become *la causa?*
there are some who are ready
to die for the revolution
but how many will live for it?

sex is either over-glorified
or underestimated
but seldom is it just sex.

it is always true
that power, knowledge, honor
make man highly complicated
and sophisticated
but in the case of true greatness
man remains simple.

the true root of all problems
is the refusal of the situation
and consequently of the role
one must play in it,
many of us go through life
wanting to be an ass
when our role was to be
an eye.

one good soldier
is worth a thousand brilliant generals
on the battlefield.

The Inn of the Seven Arts
(Better Known as the Pittman's)

smack center phoenix, palm trees
     and orange blossoms
temona awaits, the door is open,
come and rest ye poets,
musicians, painters, dancers
         and hoboes,
credentialed artists
       and aspiring fools.
arthur is playing *ajedrez*
         melissa's at ballet practice
and a daughter who denies god
plays constant and beautiful piano
music for him—
a son is away finding his own healing touch
and hal, zen-like, christ-like
carves new life for someone under a *microscopio*.
don't worry about upsetting
there serenity or the food bill
         temona's formula works well
the more she shares with others
         the more her late discovered
god goes on to share with her.
don't even say *gracias*
       and when you leave
leave the *puerta abierta*
       just as you found it.
       i was there a week
       i know.
the magii, the messiah, saint joseph,
chicanos, blacks, roamers
of all kinds and races
have found this spiritual oasis
discovered there their own hands and faces.

You

you are part of sunday
                my sunday,
                        my sunday in dallas,
my sunday *nublado*
                and your morning eyes
                                serene and dark
i drank   i penetrated
your nearness
                radiated a sun
                        of its own
and your mouth
                waiting
                        invited
                                spelled mystery
a kiss   an imaginary kiss
you caused me intimate bliss.

Ya No

ya no
        ya no quiero pintar mi verso gris
quiero pintarlo un verde rojo,
no quiero escribir más del mal
                de la miseria, del hambre
ya no—ya no
        ya no quiero escribir poemas
                        de hombres que no aman
                        y no sueñan,
                        que llevan el alma envenenada,
quiero escribir mis rimas
                de gozo, de un gozo tan dulce
                que haga que mi alma agarre lumbre
                y me broten unas lágrimas de fuego
                y con ellas caliente al mundo entero.
ya no   ya no   ya no
no quiero escribir
                de dudas y malicias
                                y de hombres ciegos
que nunca han visto a dios,
quiero convertir mis palabras
                        en sonrisas
                                en besos
                                        y abrazos
y hacer con ellas en cada amanecer una poesía.
quiero ponerle fin
                al verso triste
                        quiero que aprendamos
a amar
        y a compartir
                y a respetar.
ya no   ya no   ya no   ya   no
ya no quiero escribir
                de lo que veo sino de lo que sueño.

The Poet as a Mirror

like some people i have met and seen
with the capabilities of a human x ray machine
para el alma.
the mirror must be clean
               to capture the image well
               ah, yes . . . .there must be light
darkness allows no images
               only bulks and shadows.
a camera, an x ray machine
can capture images
with accurate fidelity
a million times better than man can.
so true
       but the poet/mirror interprets
       what's not there
       visible to the unpoetic eye.
transports he/she the image of a
               mesquite guarding the sands of a desert
and plants it in the big busy city's slum,
measures the fleeting moment-love
and makes it stand still on paper
               for the slow, the non poet
               to come and stare at
               as long as he/she wants to.
in his better moments he hunts god
and once in a while brings back
pieces of him/her like moonrocks
               for us to have instead
of bread and wine converted
and this mirror as if by
inherited magic formula
inplanted in his glass/blood soul
creates at rare moments as god did
               something out of nothing.

Happy 200th Anniversary (In Case We Get There)

u.s.a., my country, just in case you get there
and i don't, or if you weren't and i were,
let me wish you a happy 1976
and it can really be, you know.
patria pecosa and *antihigiénica,*
spraying lysol and aerosol on everything
and gargling away lies with listerine,
patria sucia envenenando el río,
the lake, the forest, the city
with factories that manufacture nothing
and cars that go nowhere.
i am one of those fools who love you,
who believe in your dream, in your soul
with freckles and pollution,
i believe in your constitution
and that thing called balance of powers,
i believe in you and in god and in santa claus.
you could indeed be great and number one,
my country, by choice and not by chance,
the rock music, the pot incense
through your many ventilators,
your giant corporation mergers,
corruption, *la mafia*, graft and
churches of christ without christ . . .
all of this could be right
as if only one of those disney
characters would wave at us
a magic wand,
if only. . . .
      here, then, is my secret
                  gift to you, i know
     how you can be
            the pride of the
                 very universe.

in those short couple of centuries
you have written your own history,
the version has you on god's right
and under the skirts of lady justice
destined to multiply democracy like germs
and spread god unto pagans
as if he were margarine
          and we couldn't
                    it is not nice to fool mother nature.
the secret is
like those freckles *en el alma*
que tenemos como pecas
from "pecatore"
a worldwide confession is in order
acknowledging the historical sins
errors, pre-meditated genocides,
robberies, broken treaties, double talk
and abuses, oppression, imperialistic deeds
and attitudes, acts of arrogance, racism,
laws written to steal and with fraudulent
intention, our selfish imposition, intervention,
and profit-chasing madnesss,
apologize to the entire world,
to mexico, korea, vietnam, *al indio, al negro,*
al chicano, al mismo blanco
only then when you and i
humbly accept we did wrong,
          que la cagamos, pues . . . .can we live in peace.
the flagwavers   who
believe such a day will never come,
that it is beyond their diginity,
the very essence of being american
is being proud, historically proud
and righteous.
those who beg off
a moment of truth
and wish to ignore the watergate *mierda,*

the pueblo incident, the u.2,
the chicano educational atrocities,
the *indio* buffalization,
the blackman's de-dignification,
the many appalachias, the treatment
of *viejitos* and veterans, the exploitation
of ten million for the sake of a few,
the *cochinadas* going on we call craft,
the slavery of farmworkers,
all these unamericans
prevent us from truly being great,
acknowledging we goofed
and feeling sorry and ashamed
for the misery we've caused
can only make us stand tall
before the very stars of heaven,
we can be then god's chosen
ground for his re-entry,
going to the moon or mars
cannot possibly equal
the heights we can reach
and at that all it takes is a president
with guts to say it to us . . . for us . . .
to the world,
then . . . three hail marys and three our fathers
and three billion dollars and a promise to sin no more
or better yet a promise to screw them all instead of pay
after all, fools like me and bigots like you love you anyway.

Espinas

there was no coffee or juice to be had
so i drank the morning instead,
it tasted of desert and sun
and satisfied me as well
                    using the windows
                    for my drinking glass
                    and the hills around for spoons
me desayuné.
seeing nopales y chile secándose al entrar
volví a ser niño otra vez
                    feeling myself very alone
me abracé de la noche anoche
                    y en aquel silencio hermoso
                    como niño también me dormí.
all this was so strange
                    to one who is usually sorrounded
                    in busy airports
                    by many many people
                              like espinas.
the noise of a jet overhead
                    reminded me
                              nearby
                                   civilization
threatened
el desierto
y la lluvia had made death valley
sprout from its dead earthy womb
the most beautiful of desert flowers
according to the color tv
                    serving the six o'clock news
and the tv don't lie
                    when it comes to desert flowers.
maybe the desert, all deserts,
                    have always been within
                    y nuestra sequía sí tiene fin.

Stephanie

so much tenderness cannot forever captive be
an so one morning early upon awakening ran free . . .
how many thousand minutes after
do i flavor (mental-tongue now) its escape,
i was, for lack of words,
touching the thoughts,
poor substitutes that they remain,
and felt the blanket night
puzzled by the once in an eternity
scenes which never do repeat
but which awaiting cues,
behind the stage of living,
alertly, predicted, do remain,
banquets of love cannot be rushed
even if the hunger so demands
and so . . . to really know
such meal must yet be taken slow
well, anything but still,
spirit, anything but tame,
child dipped in womanhood.
there . . . shivering like a frightened rabbit
frozen by floodlights,
asking forever to repeat
the question or the answer . . .
embarrassed? no . . . how can i be?
how can anybody be
embarrassed to be born?
my whole body wants to speak so i must be quiet now
only your fingers can listen . . . only they know how.

Uanetl, Indio sin Regalo

uanetl, fue uno de los últimos aztecas
que ofreció sacrificio al sol.
uanetl, no era de los nobles
y tuvo que esperar a que todos
hubieran terminado,
uanetl, no soñaba sueños bonitos
y las pocas veces que quizo
describir sus humildes aventuras
se rieron mucho de él,
el sacrificio al sol se tenía
que hacer ese día
y el sol ya empezaba a someter
su cara ardiente circular
cuando uanetl llegó a la
piedra sacrificial
al pie de la pirámide
se sintió muy solo y muy triste
y se dio cuenta que sus
manos estaban vacías
—no llevaba nada
        que ofrecer a los dioses—
de sus ojos negro-noche
brotó una lágrima
del tamaño de una gota
de agua de llovizna.
los dioses se conmovieron
y lo llenaron de bonitos
pensamientos, de sueños y palabras
y le concedieron algo muy grande
vivir escondido
en el futuro dentro de millones
        de chicanos
                en aztlán.

Envy

love itself in one of those
moments of ecstasy
                    which missed its target
impregnated humanity,
                    no, not a race
                              or a class
but humanity's womb
                    in general
                              and we were born
with the green gene
but some mutations
roam the earth
                    who rather than
                              wanting to accumulate
they share
rather than hate—they care.

From Los to Reno

lubrica mi existir con gotas de tu amor,
transforma mi frío en tu calor
y pon toda la ternura en tus dedos
y tócame, enbrújame al tocarme
con caricias tuyas
y alas de mariposas negras.
rompe el silencio con unas
                              frases dulces,
hazme saber, hazme comprender
lo incompleto que verdaderamente soy,
busca con tus labios a los míos
                            y plántales un sol
que diga un beso.
en nudo semi seda semi humano
vamos a emprender camino
                         a lo divino,
vamos a gozar la desnudez
de dos espíritus en pleno verano,
caminemos, compañera mía,
                        amante, esposa, novia, lo que seas,
aluza tú primero
                        que más tierna tienes la mirada,
ponle a mi corazón un distintivo
para que pueda bailar toda la noche,
haz que broten de mi corazón
                        con la misma frecuencia
palabras que sólo brotan de mi mente,
abrázame, apaga de una vez la sed
con tu presencia
y baña mi deseo con tu inocencia.

Cream or Sugar?

siempre, carnal, el café del vivir
        es negro y muy amargo
        sin embargo
hay su crema, su leche de bote, su *coffeemate*
y su azúcar
endulzado el café como nuestras vidas
                                sabe más suave.
mataron a mi compadre manuel
        el viernes en la cantina, la green lantern,
        lo mató un gabacho chiple
y por seguro, su papá, el influyente,
lo sacará de éste y otros líos
(ya había matado a otro cristiano hace unos años)
a mi compa, chema, le dio tres plomazos
(al otro lo navajeó)
y pa' la coma y su hijo y su jefita
        pos lágrimas negras y amargas
        como el café,
la azúcar y la crema
        en que los años juntos los vivieron
a toda,
        como una familia, chica,
                pero muy feliz,
y el compa, tan cerca de dios
                que siempre andaba,
comulgó esa mañana
                        sin saber que en la noche
lo tatemaban haciendo su deber
como un policía especial,
                        quesque cuidando la ley y el orden
nosotros sí que respetamos esas cosas
y hasta morimos por ellas
pero otros nomás hablan
porque se oye bonito hablar.

Three Margaritas Later

i already went through the weapons check
at concourse d but my head must be back
at the bar
where mario and i shared three drinks,
i, three margaritas and he, three bloody marys
he substituted, as a good chicano should,
tequila for vodka
and at a dollar-thirty a drink
plus tip we also shared some
words, some private confessions
which became more sincere and more private
after the second drink.
i wait here at gate six
my frontier jet to tucson,
i'll be an hour-and-one-half late,
everything seems to be running late
nowadays,
even death waits a bit longer
to come and claim us
among the lost and found.
mario went his way . . .
> caminos diferentes todos
> llegando a donde mismo
destiny had it . . . *futurismos* . . .
which went haywire
in the god-computer,
that i discuss
with another carnal at breakfast
my philosophy on life,
the hereafter and all that junk
in which a few nuts
like us
are interested,
the margaritas rested.

Feliz Cumpleaños, Esposa Mía

que te alcancen mi beso y mi abrazo
   felicitando el hecho que hoy es tu día,
que en la palabra mi corazón pierda un pedazo
   al decirte, feliz cumpleaños, esposa mía.

after all these years together we have learned
   to assume, without too much trouble, each other's identity
and in all these years how often i've yearned
   not to take for granted the fact that you are an entity.

es que aún después de tanto juntos
   no en verdad nos conocemos bien
y al seguir extraños los más íntimos asuntos
   quedan sin palabras en las mentes de cada uno, de cada quien.

i've often wanted to tell you how beautifully serene
   your face appears, like out of some roman cuento
particularly when to the act of love le hemos puesto fin
   but i have held the comment back, shy, lo ausento.

to remember your birth is a very private thing
   even esposos *cannot fully appreciate or share*
but i think can be thankful for your wedding ring
   tells me you were born for me to somebody care.

y que si de nuevo te digo . . . te quiero,
   cuántas veces antes ya de mi lo has oído,
mas como un ave maría que se dice por el mundo entero
   miles de veces, cada nueva vez tiene nuevo sentido.

jainita mía, *sweet*, contenta y triste compañera
   look at the sunny side of our lives, the rainbows
and hold back those ready tears, our vereda,
   i admit, is narrow but together we don't care where it goes.

From Albu to Tucson

mi bisabuela, dios la tenga en paz, andrea flores,
ciega y tullida, contaba cuentos de los mejores,
desde su humilde catre . . . su voz ya débil
desenredaba fantásticas leyendas
     y yo con la boca abierta
pequeño pero muy alerta
me le colgaba con toda mi imaginación
     y aquel aún inocente corazón,
de cada una de sus palabras.
     ella era en mi infancia, mucho antes
que se inventara la televisión,
mi zenith de 21 pulgadas . . . a colores.
allí conocí, verda' de dios que sí,
porque los miraba en mi mente
cada que ella los mencionaba,
a chucho el roto, simbad el marino,
y a juan sin miedo . . .
ese juan sin miedo sí me cuadraba
y ella con la mano temblándole mientras
prendía otro "faro" o "carmencita"
y a chupe y chupe y a cuento y cuento
y quién iba a pensar aquel entonces
que tantos años después
despertado el recuerdo quizá por los sangoloteones
de un jet
     o por unos tequilitas
yo me iba a acordar de aquella
viejecita . . . canuda y arrugada
que cuando se le secaba la boca
de tanto hablar
me decía —tráime un jarro de agua, hijito
y yo corría a la tinaja
y ese jarro de agua era el "comerical," el intermedio
y le seguíamos luego con la aventuras de juan sin miedo.

Preguntas Pesadas

for some strange reason i cannot explain
i woke up from my usual unperturbed sleep . . . again,
trying to define you . . .
        a bottle . . . that's it, one with no bottom
so that many can pour themselves into
but none can be contained within.
(poured, used here spiritually and sexually)
and since most of us are bent on our own destruction
(including and mostly you and me)
we became weapons for each other
and as weapons share no blame
in the intention of the user.
since the bottle is open at both ends
there is no room for a spirit.
can you, bottle without corks,
fall in love?   have faith?
                        be faithful?
be happy?   have a child?
that glass
       from which the bottle is made
is very sensitive,
       very sensuous
and desirable
       and it can accommodate
all
  and all can rub themselves
into the sides
       and the sides are warm
but nonetheless
made of glass.

Under the Skirt of Lady Justice
43 Skirts of Abelardo
(1978)

Requiem for an Ex CAP Director

symbolically his staff presented him
with a huge sword with which to kill a dream
which is fast turning into a nightmare.
the dream was ending poverty.
now poverty
            in the cap agencies
is multiplied and duplicated
in their expensive xerox machines.
the sword was presented
            to ralph rivera
in boulder colorado
            en la casa de los sáiz.
he was a modern don quixote
            who chased
dragons in the sky riding first class in jets.
he almost cornered the dragons
in washington, d.c.
by now, like rivera,
there are many more chicanos
who never dreamed
            of being executives
of the business of poverty.
now they are
            ex cap directors.
some are even in prisons.
others became the target of the randomly thrown
vendido label our *raza* applies to them.
rivera is but one example of those many.
he was asked to resign
because he could not conquer poverty
in the state of colorado
or improve the migrant camps
or he could not account
for forty-nine cents of his two-million-dollar budget.

maybe it was because he succeeded despite the inherited
conspiracy from within.
so . . . go and rest, rivera,
tend your sheep,
they understand
more of poverty
        than the o.e.o. sextagon in washington.
chicanos must not trade away
        their charisma
for cap forms.
chicanos must do their best
to relate their meager fundings
to the vast movement for total change.
they must refuse to become shock absorbers
with a *tetera* in their hands
to pacify the angry masses.
go, rivera, and help
tomás and facundo
        bake adobes.
build instead of leaders inanimate things.
they cost less.
go and rest.
wear well your decorations
upon your sincere heart
which only wanted to help others
but which was as foolish as any one else's
as to how to do it.
soon another one will try his hand
at fighting poverty and earning his rest.
longevity for cap directors
is a short one.
you please washington
        and fool the poor
or you fool washington
and please the poor.
the game
        has only sixty seconds.

you become a good example
of how human
        the tendency is
                to kick a man
who is down.
chicanos
        who should be coming strong
to your aid
whisper low
that they are only:
—casual acquaintances
rest in antonito,
be again a family man.
enjoy . . . repose . . . *descansa*.
drink a beer or two.
i will not, however, accept
your resignation
from the movement
        of chicanos
                on the go
who fight for first-class
        citizenship,
who want to make some rules
of their very own
as to how to play the silly sixty seconds game.
requiem for an ex cap director
who came close to being the revolution's x factor.

No Tengo Papeles

usté dispense, ¿cuál es el nombre désta ciudá?
tengo necesidá.
		no tengo papeles.
quiero trabajar.
me quiero mejorar.
		no tengo papeles.
el hambre
	no tiene fronteras
ni reconoce ríos.
		no tengo papeles.
estos lugares
por donde yo busco chamba
no me son desconocidos.
es el mismo méjico que fue robado.
			no tengo papeles.
el presidente de aquí
me quiere dar amnestía.
quisiera que en vez de eso
hiciera justicia
	con los malos sueldos
y las malas condiciones de trabajo
como yo me gano la vida.
		no tengo papeles.
tengo sed de justicia.
		no tengo papeles.
mis hermanos chicanos
me desconocen
	y me insultan.
no me abajan
	de pinche mojado
		muerto de hambre.
tengo frío. tengo miedo.
		no tengo papeles.
busco por acá

lo que en mi patria no hay
por la misma culpa
de tanta explotación americana.
por tonto que me crean
yo entiendo de economía.
tenga la razón pero
            no tengo papeles.
me echan a mi la culpa
por tanta gente
que hay aquí sin trabajo
y porque la economía estadounidense
anda por los suelos.
yo no tengo la culpa
            no tengo papeles.
la migra, ah, la migra
ese brazo elástico
del ranchero ventajoso,
del gobierno convenenciero
es el mismo que dejé atrás en méjico.
rompe mi cabeza
y me asesina
diciendo que sólo fue un acidente.
todos se lo creen.
yo tengo la verdad pero
            no tengo papeles.
lo poco que gano
a veces me alcanza
pá mandar
un quiotro dólar
a los que dejé atrás
pero no los veo llegar.
tengo una familia tan grande.
            no tengo papeles.
sí, es verdad,
la tristeza por estos rumbos
y ese idioma de los perros
es inaguantable

y en veces me emborracho
y me enamoro,
tengo corazón pero
            no tengo papeles
ni casa tengo.
mis patrones
en veces me hacen el favor
de dejarme dormir en un gallinero.
ya llevo mucho tiempo sufriendo.
            no tengo papeles.
nací sin papeles.
crecí sin papeles.
yo sé quién soy.
soy mejicano.
pido trabajo. no pido limosna.
hay otros aquí sin papeles.
a ellos nadie los molesta
porque ellos están güeros.
otros quesque le andan corriendo
            al comunismo
sí, mi espalda esta mojada
pero de sudor.
mis huevos también.
            no tengo papeles.
                  no tengo papeles.
no tengo papeles.

Anclas de Desunidad

¡qué casualidad!
para hablar de unidad
hay que hablar de división primero.
este tribuismo antiguo
es un ancla en el ombligo
no nos deja caminar.
yo soy azteca. yo soy tolteca.
chichimeca. olmeca. zapoteca. apache.
laguna. navajo. pueblo. yaqui. comanche.
siño, yo soy un probe indio lepero sin huarache.
este regionalismo antiguo
es un ancla en el ombligo
no nos deja caminar.
yo soy sureño. yo soy de la capital.
soy del valle. soy de las montañas.
yo soy de la costa. yo del *midwest*.
yo soy norteño, casi güero,
vaquero y todo ese pedo. yo soy rural.
yo soy urbano, ese,
estoy *sophisticated* de a madre.
i know where all the movidas *are*
and how to get it on.
estas divisions organizacionales
son unas anclas fatales
no nos dejan caminar.
yo soy lulac. yo soy del g.i. forum.
yo soy del project ser. yo soy image.
umas. masa. c.s.a. cufa. mecha.
u.f.w. t.f.w. a.&w.?
upward bound. h.e.p. e.o.p. p.p.p.
—ahí está el escusado en la otra puerta.
estas divisiones políticas
son unas anclas críticas
no nos dejan caminar.

yo soy *republican*. yo soy *democrat*.
yo ser del *american party*.
yo soy de la raza unida.
—¿cuál de las cuatro?
yo voy con wallace.
—ora, bruto, si wallace no está corriendo.
pos ni yo estoy votando.
estas divisiones ideológicas
son anclas ilógicas
no nos dejan caminar.
yo soy comunista. yo soy marxista.
yo soy socialista. yo so anarquista.
leninista. troikista. zapatista. ¿nudista?
nacionalista. tercer mundo. revolucionario.
reformista. alambrista. yo soy radical.
yo soy un conservador.
—Ora, pendejo, ¿qué conservas, la pobreza?
estas divisiones físicas
son unas anclas tísicas
no nos dejan caminar.
éste es güero. aquél es prieto.
éste es alto. aquél es chapo.
éste está flaco y aquél es barrigón
éste es narizón y aquél está molacho.
éste es un buen hombre y aquél es un borracho.
éste está greñudo y aquél está pelón.
éste está más feo que el carbón
y aquél tiene *sex appeal*.
estas divisiones económicas
son unas anclas cómicas
no nos dejan caminar.
éste es pobre. aquél es rico.
ésta está en *welfare*
y aquél anda atrás de las estampillas.
éste es *middle class*. tiene dos carros.
—diles la verdad, ni uno de los dos anda
éste gana un dólar arriba del *poverty guidelines*.

éste está en *unemployment*.
—oh, no yo no estar en *unemployment*.
yo ser un *consultant* en *unemployment*.
estas divisiones hijas de puta
son un ancla bruta
          no nos dejan caminar.
yo soy chicano. yo soy mejicano.
yo soy *mexican american*. yo soy *spanish*.
yo soy mojado. yo soy manito. yo soy pocho.
yo soy estudiante. yo soy campesino.
soy mariguano. soy tecato. soy bato loco.
y yo soy pinto.
yo ser un *program director*.
—eres un vendido.
el vendido fue tu padre.
yo soy joven. tú estás viejo.
—vieja la luna, güey.
yo soy del *gay liberation*.
yo soy del *women's liberation*.
—ora, vieja chirinolera, póngase a amasar.
sí, mis queridos carnales,
aunque tenemos muchas cosas que nos hacen diferentes
todos tenemos una cosa en común.
todos estamos bien jodidos
y para dejar de estar jodidos hay que estar unidos.

From Frisco to Fresno

pasa, viejo amigo, a platicar conmigo un rato.
el tiempo es nuestro y el vino es aún barato.
a poor pale example of a man
beat up on a woman night before.
that *muy macho* wanted to settle the score
and bruised, half-dying, she was left
in the street . . . in the night
to heal herself, to go back to him
and love him even more, to run in fear, to implore.
come, old friend, let us talk a while.
it is our own time we waste. let's drink and smile.
they are nearing the impeachment
            of a despot king
who was not satisfied with merely being great,
he wanted to be supreme.
let's hope they tape the mess up
and restore a bit of confidence
in the social shambles of a nation
which once had the potential
            of becoming a second paradise.
pasa, amiga/querida,
            mi casa es tu casa.
deja que tiemblen
            nuestros cuerpos una vez más.
esta vez de despedida.
let me as i bite gently your lip
go on and wish you a safe trip.
you go to central america,
to nicaragua, you say.
you are catching a ride
to what you believe to be
the expansion and growth
of your very soul.
as i said before . . . *buen viaje.*

enter, companion of a long time,
the champagne is flowing.
i want in a brief toast
        to tell you
                you are strong and self-sustaining.
drink one more glass
        and drown your fears.
                imaginary or real,
                        of dying,
of being left alone, of going insane.
dear woman of mine,
don't you see that only then
you would be in step
with the rest of the world
which long ago lost its own head?
come in, friend, spit out your anger
at my face.
fermented angry spit
can also get us drunk.
you're sore
because i made love,
a few times and in a hurry, to your ex wife.
is your anger at me
because you see me now
in the splendor of my shiny dishonesty
which has turned me into a full-size mirror
in which you see yourself?
come in, *te he estado esperando,*
estás flaca . . . muy flaca,
puro hueso ya sin alma
caminando solo
        con el soplo de algún viento.
i do not offer you anything to drink.
you do not like tea, coffee or juice
or a lime-cold drink from arctic circle.
i offer you instead my own blood.
suck it out and make me skinny like you.

pero por dios
¡si es el mismo dios
que viene a verme!
maybe he can explain to me
el hormiguero que hay en mi cuerpo.
maybe he can tell me
in which *volcán* originated
the lava/desire which makes me
look at any female standing in front of me
as a living target.
i'll just have a glass of milk
in which to dunk
my last hard on.
pasa, pasa tú también,
         diablo pinche,
que la casa de mi alma
es bastante grande.
aquí tengo un fuerte aguarraz
         para brindar contigo
your last subdivision
as hell surely has by now
         its slums and its suburbias.
better yet, this night i will drink alone
una leche pálida de un pálido pezón.

The Last Wow

the blue-eyed gypsy is gone.
once again i'm all alone.
there is no song. there is no poem.
gypsies must move on
or else they won't be gypsies long.
the last wow,
the last *ajúah*
      have been said.
the drops of dew, sweat and love
fell on each other one last time.
siamese souls of love
cannot be
      dissected with words
without real blood erupting
as if invited by a knife.
—i want to travel some more,
abroad . . . here,
do some growing up.
i refused, my ears refused,
to listen anymore,
to be a witness
to the tears of anguish
spoiling the beauty of your face
which is by now a permanent fixture in my mind.
i chose instead to listen
      to the song we call our own
and relive those moments
of one of our many honeymoons.
—*tanto tiempo disfrutamos de este amor.*
nuestras almas se acercaron tanto así
que yo guardo tu sabor
pero tú llevas también, sabor a mí.
the zodiac,
    the many horoscopes we read each other,

the gemini and the sagittarius,
they approved of our love
and made such sound
and healthy predictions.
the lines in the palm of my hand
        confirmed
the duality of my joy,
our joy.
numerology . . . the number seven,
echoed in envious applause our heaven,
the find each was to each other.
inside a church
when we received
holy communion together
we thanked god for our love/sin.
we had by then settled
all the major differences which,
futuristically speaking,
had our meeting and falling in love
in the realm
of possibilities
that happen only
on a zillion to one basis.
how is it then
        that now
                a last wow
                        brings sudden death
to our love just as it flowered,
challenging tradition
and daring to establish itself
in the testing grounds of immorality?
i sing some more in the silence of my mind
trying to escape the sadness of the moment:
—*yo no sé si tenga amor la eternidad*
pero entonces como aquí
en tu boca llevarás sabor a mí.
the last wow.

what is a wow?
you and i already know
but does the originator of such a sound
centuries ago
        mind our using
his shout of joy
brought about by spiritual explosions
dispersing sensuously all the feathers
in our bodies?
wow is our personal no-meaning sound
manifesting our happiness.
—you are so final.
can you leave the door open? —you asked.
you added, —gypsies have been known to return.
i said to myself, —ghosts do not bother with doors.
those who are already inside need no doors to come in.
the last wow
is a mortal blow
which somehow, as you already know,
takes love/life away.
the last wow is the last everything.
the blue-eyed gypsy is gone.
once again i'm all alone.
there is no song. there is no poem.
gypsies must move on
or else they won't be gypsies long.

—*pasarán más de mil años, muchos más* . . .

Wife

among other things
you married a pair of wings.
do not clip them.
climb on and fly.
while dreams are known the world over,
of course,
 you married the source.
don't try
to understand him.
the task is big.
who knows,
 the reward
  may not be worth the effort.
you married
someone who'd much rather
understand suffering
than console.
one who will ignore pain
 and tears
his and others'.
one who behaves
like an ostrich
at the sight of trouble
 but who will readily
 sacrifice all
or yield nothing,
one whose sense
of value is
either ignoring truth
or warped realism.
one whose religion
is as hollow

                    as a plaster statue
                              or as solid as
                                        the touch

or morning dew upon the green.
you married
a paper sack
with lots of holes
containing faith.
what's more
you married someone
          who flatly
refuses to sit in the back.
one who dreams so high
one who feels at home
in the simple darkness
of nobodyness.
the one you married
          worships
the brightness of the mind
and will not worry
if the house
burns down tomorrow
or the soul forever.
one whose insanity
may have its roots
          in loneliness.
yes, the one who is your mate
will die early
and live late.
in his nothingness
          you can pan
the gold dust
          of being great.
while he may not agree with you
or compliment you
or feel sorry for you
          he will do more.
he will understand.

while he will never be
a father
        or a husband
he will fill those roles
by merely being himself.
to say you have him,
to say you found him,
to say he is yours
        will only please your ears
because if it were
        that he would belong to you
or to anyone else
he would be lost.
to share your life with a puzzle
was your "i do"
his
        (and this is
                your only
                        real satisfaction)
has lasting value galore
for his love is a never empty store.

La Barraca

opening night, the beer isn't cold yet.
november twelve . . . i bet we'll soon forget.
yet,
      when four very determined chicanos
go on business together
and open a bar
      in the middle of the texas desert
near mission
it can be taken
      as a declaration
of independence.
a vintage jukebox
blasts vintage chicano *rancheras y corridos*.
the first customers,
lalo, lucas, lupe *y* rené . . .
los dueños: pablo rubén *y* samuel
tend bar and drink away the profits.
marcos lópez, *sí señor*, joins the group
and others come in to the opening occasion.
—set up the first round.
—*pongan las otras,*
      yo las pago.
the fourth owner of the "establishment"
is away in philadelphia.
he is narciso alemán.
i receive two unexpected compliments:
—i was looking forward to meeting you.
i remember many lines from your poems.—
words paying for words.
sincerely said, i'm sure.
i wish them *suerte en su empresa*
and toast away their economic venture.
more than a cantina
it is a *cuartel*
para los chicanos de acción
que piden revolución.

What Is Life?

hilda, bert and roberto complied
in sharing with me *a sábado de gloria* which had died
only a couple of hours before.
we kept vigil on the last day of our ten-day fast.
we tossed and turned
       trying to find the soft side of the hard floor
where we laid.
we had plenty of conversation,
       light and wise, we spoke of many things.
we also listened to portions of the album,
jesus christ, superstar.
just as we all were getting pretty sleepy
roberto posed the question, —what is life?
he repeated it,
       afraid that i had missed it, —what is life?
then the most beautiful thing happened.
just as i tried
       a series of abelardistic
(after me, not the other abelard)
          attempts at what at 2 a.m.
of easter 1972
       could be considered
          damn well satisfying answers,
i began to hear heavy snoring.
my three friends had gone to sleep
       and could care less
for my brilliant answer to such a philosophical question.
the beautiful thing being
that they did not wait for the answer.
not waiting for the answer only proves
trying to define life is hard. it won't stand still. it moves.

Scumble

to scunner and not to hate,
to scupper and keep the taste,
to hide under the thick scurf
of scurrile life that yearning
to scurry itself leaps out
and is able to see its own scut,
obsolete as old scutage.
scutched, then, my mountainous love
with the scutcheon of no hope
my nonhoping scute hides me.
pour, fate, then, into my scuttle
so that i can scuttle away my love.
i still have faith as scutum
tho time's scythe cuts away my autumn.

De Corpus a San Antonio

it is rather strange
that in the english language
no word rhymes with orange.
in spanish no word rhymes with naranja?
it's just as well. i did not mean
to rhyme it with anything anyway.
if i did
        i would probably
invent a word myself,
coin one myself.
"florange" as an example.
florange would be my word
for the flower of the orange,
for the orange blossom.
what good
        is my poetic license
if i never get to use it?
because english is my second language
the endings of english words
keep throwing me off . . . way off.
i rhyme love with job
and orange would rhyme with change or ranch
or even range.
they all sound the same to my chicano ear.
despite the "b" i got in my phonetics class
when i was making speech my minor
back in my college days
english sounds are foreign.
what fuss, huh?
        fiddling around
with the intricacies of communications,
poetic and otherwise,
which, after all, don't suffice worth a shit
to make soul to soul communication . . . complete?

The I.A.

hunger is the modus operandus.
exploitation is de facto to all of us
to use apropo terminology.
if the honorable chairman of these hearings
yields the floor to a chicano for a minute
i will elaborate on what appears to me
to be a well-plotted cons-pi-ra-cy:
—cheap labor to maximize the margin of profits.
a nation unable to house and feed its citizens.
the seed in us to abuse the unprotected weak.
an uncaring, unconcerned, apathetic public.
a legislative body
              burdened by many priorities.
put all these elements together
and you have eight million undocumented workers
all around you.
they do make a nice size scapegoat for all
the economic woes facing our nation.
why, what can be more unamerican than to have
the highest rate of unemployment
and play deaf and blind to these "illegal aliens"?
let me propose some solutions
              to the problem:
—open up the borders.
occupy mexico. send gabachos to look for work in mexico.
declare all i.a.s. a communist threat.
make it all an international harvest game.
marry them off to every available u.s. dame.

Alternative Ed

one battleground where the front
continues to swallow up chicanos like a *pinchi* cunt
is the establishing of our own schools,
no matter, be they preschool
     or postgraduate.
the blessings of accreditation
are only dispensed by an anglo pope.
there is really no hope.
u.c.l.i. jacinto treviño, tlatelolco,
colegio de la tierra, juárez lincoln, d.q.u..,
colegio césar chávez,
     etcetera . . . etcetera.
the funds with which we must perform miracles
continue to be such,
really not too much
     to even buy pencils
or toilet paper.
pero le seguimos dando gas.
un día lagañozo en fresno
     under the roof of a condemned building
unos cuantos chicanos
que son como las baterías del sears
que se llaman diehard
se juntaron to continue their dream
of diplomas *con el* shape *de tortillas,*
de no tener que comprar nuestra educación de rodillas
ni con estampillas . . .
lo nuestro es sueño y es también trabajo,
siguen siendo así mientras seamos los de abajo.

De Harlingen a Corpus

descendants of *príncipes aztecas* in south *tejas*,
sensitive to *la raza*'s historic, painful, constant *quejas*,
plan a pyramid to the sun,
       la pirámide del sol.
where they can offer sacrifice again
          a los dioses.
there, they will sacrifice ignorance, hunger,
racism, oppression and disease.
it will be a place where our own history
will be displayed in bright hues
upon its murals.
there our own chicano college will be housed.
thousands of chicanos can come to share,
to hope, to build, together at one time.
it is sad we must wind up pricing
such a needed monument,
the symbol of our own monumental despair,
must be measured and tagged
      in dollars and in cents.
seven million dollars . . . more or less . . .
a projected date of five years . . .
qué sueño,
     ¿verdad, carnales?
mayas and *aztecas* had such dreams.
now real pyramids still stand
where they once dreamed.
they built at even greater sacrifice
a legend to leave us for posterity in *piedra bruta.*
is our mission less important than theirs?
that pyramid will stand on, and look accusingly,
tierras que nos robaron,
the same *tierras* our *tatarabuelos* desraizaron.

The Willing and Unwilling Victims

how much coitus has been accrued,
how the migrant is being screwed
is of the newest in sex . . .
through the rear, through the mouth,
through the underarms . . .
so many hard ons,
(periodic reporting forms . . .
money spent . . . kids sick . . . breakdown . . .)
the migrant is developing holes all over
his body for sadistic growers
and sugar companies,
       senile crewleaders,
pimping field men . . .
worse than whores on overtime,
laws are being passed
over him, under him, around him
and through him,
ah, but that's not all
a machine is also after him
thinking
       his brown ass
          is a potato
it wants to pick it.
death seems the only escape
and so he'll die in texas,
somewhere in elsa,
somewhere in falfurrias,
but even death won't come before
more misery is inherited,
behind one more dollar merited.

Sixteen

you look back for both of us. i can't.
my eyes are clouded with a tender sentiment.

i want to remember highlights of
a ceremony that fell short of our true love.

. . . and yet, sixteen years later i see
by my side, my woman, the other part of me.

. . . and i'm filled again with gratitude.
i show the falling snow my thankful attitude.

let us talk about the score instead
of looking back and rejoice for things ahead.

we are still together. that does count.
seven children add up to quite an amount.

don't wish to recall happy events.
tears and pains are our marriage's lasting true cements.

i am not one to measure love and joy
in terms of years. they are things time cannot destroy.

Those Temporary Labor Camp Blues

to hear growers through their organization representatives
sing,
oops, i mean testify before osha, without guitar or violin,
the sadness of their song brings sudden tears.

—the economics of the whole thing —they begin,
—we already have adequate codes.
uh? local and state, that is.
we do not need the feds.
migrants are not forced to live in those camps.
they can live elsewhere if they want to.
housing does not come with the job.
why, if it becomes economically unfeasible
we will shut down the camps.
you know that all of this is forcing us
to bring about mechanization that much sooner.

if standards are not enforced
it really doesn't matter which are applied.

—the size of the room is adequate.

the flies are adequate.
the nonexistent toilets are adequate.
the lack of privacy is adequate.
but who defines "adequate"?
where, pray tell, are the affected parties?
they are in the fields, working, of course.
they are not in the forum room of the eugene hotel
in eugene, oregon,
        that's for sure.

—i grew up in a place close to a barn
and look at me, i am quite healthy.

hotels do not want the migrants
because they tear up the place.
says the wife of a grower.
more tears, my lord.
for god's sake, change the damn attitudes
and screw the regulations
for temporary labor camp violations.

De Macalitos a Harlingen

la cábula is one of our best chicano ways
of maintaining our sanity among so many strays.
lupe rivera *del valle de tejas* must be, without a doubt,
el rey de la cábula.
cuenta el lupe
       about the one time he and other *carnales*
were returning from a meeting in denver,
by plane, of course,
eran unos cinco batos
       militants . . . *pesados*, heavy, you know.
in order to catch the plane
they had missed their lunch.
traían un hambre canija del cien.
fortunately they were told they would be served
on board . . . *sigue contando el lupe*
con interruptions *del buen* rubén saenz,
que no se queda muy atrás pá esto de la cábula,
contar cracas, echar mosca,
       inventar mamadas . . .
the first thing they saw
on their food trays
       was a huge salad bowl
con su respective dressing *de* thousand islands.
le entraron duro a la ensalada.
all of the sudden *uno de ellos para de comer y les dice,*
—this is no union lettuce, *esos.*
le contestó el otro con sus bigotes
llenos de dressing,
—*vamos a* 31,000 feet up
you want to stage a walkout? just eat and shut up.

The Poor Have Now a Voice: Stereophonic at That

the thermometer of tolerance broke down
as soon as the nightgown
was removed from lady poverty
        by opportunity.
the aspirations of the poor,
thank god, kennedy, johnson, nixon or carter,
have now been lifted.
new legislation
        and meager appropriations,
i'm afraid,
are not going to be enough
or come in time
to catch the skinny malnutritioned bunch
who having tasted the filet mignon
        of our society
now want dessert.
nay . . . not only dessert
but cash
so they can give the poor underpaid waitress
a fat tip.
screw self-help housing.
we (it is now profitable and convenient
for us to associate ourselves with the poor)
want to hire
        our own draftsman,
contractor and landscaper.
we are, of course, only talking of our winter resorts
for we still migrate in the summers to pick crops of sorts.

The Group

all the efforts we now make,
our mini experiments integrating, will shake
the birth pains loose
      for a new era.
there is a new set of freedoms waiting,
impossible perhaps in years past,
highly possible in the here and now.
these freedoms,
      these sacred mushroom visions
call for us to live . . . to be human,
to love . . . to be divine,
to feel . . . to make others feel,
to share . . . to graciously receive,
to contribute . . . to care,
to respect . . . to understand.
are we capable, healthy
      juicy, erect, sex organs
capable of such
      ovum-sperm,
          spiritual encounter
and creation?
 . . . we are the group . . . the new group,
the rusty gears
thrown randomly clicking harmoniously now.
aloof history has arrived
with the blueprints
for a tomorrow heavenly utopious,
for a concern for each other abundantly copious.

Wow

—wow—you can say that again.
our emotions cooled and culled in a rain
of softness.
an ancient
        sacred law was broken.
it was
        the chance of a lifetime.
—now or never,
you should have said,
—now and always,
all clocks stop
        when happiness is stolen.
—wow—i kept saying.
it is but the noise
an animal
makes when
he is at peace with himself.
a night of bliss
capped
        a holy day.
it makes me wonder
if all life
is not really worth
one moment of sleep
in someone else's arms,
to feel healthy,
to feel good.
the word love
was never mentioned.
it was in your pink cave sanctioned.

Updated Prayers for Novochristians

lord,
keep me in good standing with the board.
guard me, o' god, from the evils of the system.
lead me not into bureaucracy.
let me recognize hypocrisy.
keep my eyes away from mini skirts.
do not let all of my bills sink me any deeper.
watch out for me for that *movida* they call the sleeper.
enlighten me to know the difference
between the bad and the good guys
and protect me from the lure of the good buys.
as i join with other war on poverty vets
keep me safe as we travel on those super jets
to attend conferences on conferences.
if nothing else keep my nose clean
and issue me a new *ángel de la guardia*
which in english means bodyguard.
shut my mouth
            and let it not indulge in controversy.
let me celebrate one more wedding anniversary
despite those many curvy young distractions.
guide me in my doubts about the pill,
the right to kill
            and the extracurricular matrimonial thrill.
keep me from uphill.
since i'm already old keep me from a fast downhill.
make me, jesus, humble and simple
in the midst of sharp computers.
make my life-rod soft and loose
to try out my new pair of florsheim shoes.

My Unborn Sons or Daughters

flowering words,
not yet sure
of their gender
or their meaning,
ovulate in me.
they crowd the shelves
of my unused mind.
they rattle now and then
     only
to remind
     themselves and i
that they exist
ready to describe
some new emotions,
some distant days,
some smiling faces.
for now they sleep
as i have trivia to keep.

Padre Island, Ten A.M.

chicanos meet while nearby waves roar.
they meet to settle among themselves a score.
de león sets the stage.
de la cruz speaks his piece.
uriega, lópez and barrientos
make a stand upon the sand.
"gabino" barrera, council for the defense,
isn't at all happy with what's being said.
efraín is the center of attention.
tigre scratches his head . . . he can't understand.
in the midst of the brown commotion
a couple of cars driven by some gabachos
get stuck in the sand.
        they seek help.
the whole congregation of chicanos *asoleados*
join forces to push them out
            of their trouble.
together the task is a whiz.
perhaps that is the one lesson
they came there to learn.
g.i. forum is present.
youth and maturity,
phoniness and sincerity,
the committed ones and the sellouts,
all are here . . . rivera is there from colorado
along with tafoya, alemán and delgado,
mayo . . . the tutors . . . mapa . . .
all of them gathering seashells.
historically this meeting means only one thing:
chicanos get pretty restless in the spring.

Bilingual State

while looking down on dallas
por la ventana cerca de las alas
of a trans texas jet
decidí que no sería muy bueno
to return texas to mexico
para los chicanos en estados unidos.
anyway, mexico does not want texas anymore.
yo veo
        what the wealth of texas can do
y me pregunto que cómo ha sido
that such a wealth has been accumulated . . .
no me sabe muy bien la respuesta.
dallas, houston, san antonio, corpus,
austin, laredo *y* el paso
are like little islands in a sea of land.
quizá la historia misma endureció el corazón
of the citizens of texas
y hoy sufrimos todos la rigidez
of that constipated heart.
se me viene a la mente el insulto
of that ugly huge statue at the dallas airport
y me da mucho coraje:
—one riot one ranger—
—secession from the union in 1970
me parece muy buen lema.
it is a very worthy campaign.
después de eso pedirle ayuda a los u.s.
in the name of the deprived texans
que por alguna razón extraña son
mexican-american migrants in a prison of their own.

Leftovers

in the great american cuisines
the leftovers are rice, corn, watermelon and beans.
the american eye has always been hungry for profit
and not for food.
it has overlooked
the rich value of these foods.
kentucky fried chicken,
        mcdonalds hamburgers
and shakey's pizzas
        and all the chefs and cooks
have never quite gotten around
to throwing out these foods
and those foods are spoiling fast
and stinking up the *cocina*.
they contribute to the good taste
of caviar, filet mignon,
        and baked alaska.
the leftovers
pile up in the big pots
of major cities.
burgers and hot dogs by the mountain
and coca cola by the rivers
keep confusing the gourmets.
the leftovers
        accumulate
and become the societal slop for symbolic pigs.
the leftovers will add up
until they drive out the cooks and the diners out
or until the taste for warmed-up leftovers
is developed
and all americans are by this slop enveloped.

En la Cantina

as the beer crown forms 'tween your lips and it a moat
a verse over whispers, freely but accurately, will float.
a night like this is stolen
        from *la vieja españa*
donde lorca se quejaba.
tonight is a night
to rape the muse with gusto.
it is a night to jerk
        from *el otro mundo*
sonnets the *maestro* shakespeare
never got around to writing.
here, on this notorious missouri *domicilio,*
the minds of poets light up some candles
and throw the windows wide open
so that the breeze of noble inspiration
can dance wildly with the curtains
while the verse does a striptease.
here for a few hours we stop being chicanos
or anglos and embrace each other
        in our created world
of rhyme without reason
or reason without rhyme.
la cantina is either the womb
or it is the sperm itself
which fully alive wiggles and weaves
coplas to a wife . . . *a querida* . . .
an amigo . . . a raza . . . or to *la cantina.*
vamos, que el verso sea fuerte y la bebida fina.

Christian Mythology

at one time there were upright talking snakes.
give or take some years, it very little difference makes.
        the thing is
                that there are still such vipers
        without their conscience-wipers
        that speak or hiss.
        my prayer is
                that i may learn to interpret
        what they are saying.
        folklore of that nature
        goes on to claim
        that once man
        was given domain
                of land, sea, animals,
        air, papers, machines,
        hunger, pain and knowledge.
        in a million years
        of proving that he does
        actually control all of this
        he still does not believe it.
        the glorious fairytale goes much further
        in that one father
        went on to sire
                every human being
                        probably by discharging
        cosmic cum
                upon a very sexy universe
        but that one bit of fantasy
        extends to speak of brotherhood
        and there's where the tale gets misunderstood.

De San Vicente de las Ciénegas
(Silver City) a Alburque

. . . to the puberty rites at dulce . . . yeah.
land of the apache, *mi bisabuelo* . . . yeah.
last night we surprised
a proud *señora* with *las mañanitas.*
it was only proper to share such joy
with a *carnal's jefita.* yeah.
la sally *y su guitarra*
echándole a la noche
la canción y la alegría. yeah.
i said,
—in many places they talk
about chicano culture.
here, they live it. yeah.
with a strong tail wind
            behind us
we will hit *la ciudad del duque*
                    pretty soon.
mi cajita con chile
güero, verde y colorado
va marcada como baggage . . .
a care package for salt lake . . . yeah.
i had a chance to give a quick *saludo*
to raul ruiz and an *abrazo a* freda
y warneck *de despedida.*
three more days of my life,
or sharing and stealing away
the energy of souls to stay alive one more day.

At Steve's

we chicanos are highly adaptable to all.
take these temperatures that freeze the soul
this monday night at seve's
here in monte vista
co
lo
ra
do.
my *carnales y carnalas del* c.m.c.
are celebrating the fact
that they are very, very tired
from working their asses off
to serve the *navajitos* and *chicanitos*
attending the potato harvest.
tonight there is *pachanga,*
birria, food and plenty of *pisto.*
we will throw some *chancla*
while outside
the windows in their cars
cover with frost.
we eat some
en
chi
la
das
made with new mexican *chile*
muy picoso como ellos . . . como eloy, gloria and tommy
y el jim *y el* leonard, levy, mart and lupe,
mary, domey, annie, jo ann, dorothy, estella,
herlinda, viola, peggy, roland, phillip, pat, leo
and angie and helen, cora, juanita and ronica.
we bet you anything this is aztlán and not america.

Ambassador

without the course properly drawn
i go to where i have never gone
hoping to spread
      my brand
            of truthful bull
just to watch, only once at least,
the sparkle
in the eyes of one
i have just
whispered love.
i go expecting to hear
laughter running freely.
my embassy has had
      many broken windows
and burned flags
because something
happened once
that delayed my joyful journey.
it must have been that time
that there was a shortage
of divine fuel.
now i, too,
must linger
in the lonely noise
of night
      and wait for the love word
my ears have never heard.

Parliamentary Procedure

some of your arguments are already prehistoric
so the chair will not recognize any more rhetoric.
—madam chairman.
the chair recognizes the reverend martin luther king.
—i move that we overcome.
is there a second to that motion.
—*yo la secundo.*
it has been moved and seconded
that we overcome. discussion?
—*señora presidenta.*
the chair recognizes ché guevara.
—*yo quiero amender la propuesta*
agregándole . . . a balazos.
is there a second to the amendment?
silencio.
the amendment dies for lack of a second.
the kennedies raised their hands
but ghandi was already up and speaking.
—i wish to speak for the motion.
peace
        is sought with peace.
mao and ho got up.
go on and speak, either one of you.
—history, or rather this meeting
is already taking too long.
we will never accomplish anything without violence.
—madam chairman.
yes, delgado.
—madam chairman, i call for the question.

Desde Billings hasta Salt Lake

números, números, números . . .
unos, cuatros, sietes y ceros.
los números gobiernan el universo
y todo lo que en él exista
            y todo, todo, todo.
¿cuántos millones más de mejicanos
esperas producir, oh patria mía?
¿cuántos kilos de maíz le tocan
a cada panza prieta?
números, números, números . . .
¿cuántos cuesta una medalla de oro
en la olimpiada del ochenta?
¿cuántos días hasta que venga la muerte?
¿cuántos,
            cuate mío?
¿cuántos años tiene ella?
¿cuántas veces te has enamorado?
¿cuánto ganas?
            ¿cuánto sueñas?
                        ¿cuánto cuestas?
números, números, números
números en el reloj,
            en la lotería,
en la camisa del preso,
en el seguro social,
en el buzón,
            en la computadora,
en el *zip code*
            y el *area code*
            y el *code code*
y en el tamaño de las chichis
            y de la cintura
y de las pulgadas del hombre
que le dan
            placer a la mujer.

puros números, puros pinches números
y dios, el número uno
siempre riendo con sus veinte y cinco dientes
y su par de lentes.

From Garden City to Hays

i'm going to dedicate this poem to all the liars,
sellers and buyers
           of altered truths
who early in the morning gargle with scope or listerine
so that their lies come out fresh and clean.
i'm going to dedicate this poem to all the politicians,
dead bodies and morticians
                  so they can form
a new alliance, a new party.
i'm going to dedicate this poem to all the potheads,
old old women with wrinkles and teenyboppers with
                  blackheads.
This poem is dedicated to those growing grass in the attic,
in the shower, in beer cans under heat lamps,
to all of the teachers who need to toke up
to face the students
and to the students who need to *toquearse*
to face the teachers . . .
to policeman to face the criminals,
to criminals to face the judge
and to the judge to face them both.
i'm going to dedicate this poem to the feminists,
those female nemesis
                  ready to man . . . oops . . .
the world's helm.
may our utility poles rest in peace.
i'm going to dedicate this poem to all scapegoats,
brown-nosers and turncoats,
militants, pacifists, guerilla fighters,
mercenaries and moonlighters.
you just wait and see
if this poem is not also dedicated to you.
i'm also going to dedicate it
to the gay liberationists,

matachines, bellydancers, macho pigs,
undocumented workers,
          union organizers,
program directors,
          consultants
                    and visionary
members of vice squads.
i'm going to dedicate this poem . . .
wait a goddamn minute. *con un cabrón.*
se acabó el papel.
                    there is no more room
for the so-called clumsy poem.
the damn dedication got a little too long.
there is only room to say . . . so long.

Madre

madre es una palabra que lo dice todo.
madre es lo que la vida lleva como apodo.
madre es la mitad de mi cuerpo que camina al cielo.
madre es en el desierto del vivir un pedazo de hielo.
madre es la mano tierna que toca mi frente.
madre es ejemplo de lo que es decente.
su vientre es dulce costal que produce vida.
su mirada es tierna cual paloma herida.
su palabra es vara que indica vereda
y su alma en pena es lo que uno hereda.
madre es la palabra antigua que nos habla a todos.
madre es la señora de los buenos modos.
por las venas de una madre corre un amor muy rojo.
aun hay sonrisa en su mueca con que enseña enojo.
en su pelo blanco ya un libro se ha escrito.
cada que sufre la falta de un hijo el cielo da un grito.
se termina el mundo cuando llora la falta de un hijo.
ella es la manta blanda con que mi dolor cobijo.
ella es el bocado de sustento que me da mi aliento.
ella es la oración sincera que desparrama el viento.
que tonto es uno con querer brindarle
en tan sólo un día lo que un siglo no podemos darle.
no hay pago, regalo, poema, tarjeta ni flor
que diga lo entero de su incomparable amor.
todos sabemos lo que es una madre y aún no podemos
poner en palabras sentimientos que no tienen extremos.
tampoco podemos escribir con palabras por bellas que sean
lo que es una madre para que otros vengan y lean.
quizá una madre es una bandera que a victoria lleve.
quizá una madre sea un grano de arena de importancia leve.
quizá una madre es el mismo sol que levanta al árbol.
quizá una madre sea una estatua vestida de mármol.
con nuestra madre la vida se nos hace más bella.
sin ella podemos comprender lo distante de una estrella.

como meta el resto de mi triste vida voy a dedicarme
con toda mi inteligencia en tan sólo una cosa a educarme
a ver si así estudiando tanto pueda llegar algún día
a comprender lo que es y cuánto vale esta madre mía.

La Violencia

en esta violencia yo estoy
completamente en la oscuridad . . . ya me voy.
tengo miedo
       encender un fósforo
en medio de tanto explosivo.
el ser ciudadano
              de un país
                  que almuerza,
come y cena violencia
no me deja seguir inmóvil.
hay violencia en el pensamiento
que con impulsos mortales . . . venenosos,
trauma, odio, prejuicio, racismo
e infecta en sus propias olas
al más pacífico, al más manso.
estoy entre razas heridas con sus espaldas
a una pared social.
estas arañan, maldicen, patalean,
muerden al opresor, al domador
de leones con guantes blancos
y una vara de choques eléctricos.
hay una violencia tipo "a"
y es súper superior, que mata
con sonrisas y dólares
       a naciones enteras.
esta violencia mata culturas enteras.
lo hace usando como armas
actitudes falsas y diplomas en blanco.
yo, simple tonto, producto
          de mi día,
queriéndome establecer,
laico entre expertos, les gano a la mejor
porque mi arma es más potente . . . es un violento amor.

El Corrido de Ft. Lupton

en el campo de migrantes
de ft lupton, colorado
los chicanos militantes
le hicieron raya al condado.

valenzuela hizo la punta.
goyo no se quedó atras.
lo que la raza hace junta
no solos lo harán jamás.

sánchez terminó el borlote
por viviendas adecuadas.
no fueron de su deleite
las condiciones fregadas.

el gobernador no supo
ponerle al sufrir las riendas.
recuerdo cuando yo escupo
la autoridad de viviendas.

mason fue un consejero mamón.
llegó hasta cambiar de color
al darse cuenta que el güero
nunca comprende el dolor.

recordarán en la historia
a ft lupton y al chicano
y aprenderán de memoria
que ahí se cerró la mano.

En Billings También

—dondequiera se tuestan habas
en billings las hembras son muy bravas
también y muy machos los señores.
se siente la alegría y se sienten los dolores.

un sábado en el mes aquel de agosto
decíamos que la miseria todavía se vende al costo.
pérez, lula, lalo, waldie, beto y los dos jesuses
trataban de aluzar salida con más brillantes luces.

el club latino y líderes sin nombre todavía
escuchaban lo que con mucho ánimo se discutía.
se trataba de alientar la mente y el corazón,
de buscarle a la injusticia una justa razón.

me senté y cerré por un momento mis ojos.
brevemente soñé en unos sueños muy rojos
donde el mejicano, el latino o chicano viviera
con dignidad y su labor se reconcociera.

hablamos de ayudar al campesino inmigrante.
se trata de acción pronta y no dejarlo pa' más delante.
—formaremos un concilio de una mezcla que sea buena
donde siempre se respete la opinión ajena.

De Los Angeles a Fresno

¿a dónde vas?
ya tiré mi disfraz
          y me han crecido
las alas,
voy a estrenarlas.
¿a dónde vas?
voy a borrar todas las huellas
de un pasado que desconozco.
voy como un mosco
atraído por unos granos de ázucar.
¿a dónde vas?
voy a la orilla del capitalismo
en busca de la plasma plástica
que late demasiados intereses.
¿a dónde vas?
voy al fondo del placer
o de la locura ya que son lo mismo.
voy a morder en besos
          esa droga nueva
para que se mueva
mi lento espíritu en ritmo con el universo
¿a dónde vas?
voy a la muerte
y con suerte
          que encuentre
ahí también la vida.
voy al barranco inmortal
con mis huaraches de nopal.

La Ciudad del Cañón

este lugar de mi mundo está nombrado
la ciudad del cañón del estado de colorado.
aquí las tardes se me hacen noche
y mis días no tienen broche.

la sociedad cobra caro y no se olvida
hicieron este rincón pa' darle al rencor cabida.
llevo tanto tiempo aquí que ya se me olvidó mi crimen.
lloro tanto aquí que ya mis lágrimas se esprimen.

este mundo oscuro sin niños ni mujeres
se clava en mi pensamiento como finos alfileres.
el calendario y el reloj son dos de mis enemigos.
del sufrir que yo siento los guardias son mis testigos.

que libre me siento preso.
que preso me siento libre.
pa' un hombre de buen calibre
no hay prisión de su tamaño
pero para el cobarde basta sólo con un paño.

no gasto mi tiempo aqui
y yo creo que en realidad nada es lo que yo perdí.
con mi mente salgo afuera
cada que mi mente quiera.

somos reos bien numerados,
somos hombres ya fichados.
con estas rejas frías nuestro pasado han borrado
mas el "yo" de mi persona entero se me ha quedado.

Friday 12-16-77

Qué vida, Mindy!

from one airplane into another. I am now on my way to El Paso. I'll get to see little Amanda, my granddaughter. I am on my way to pick up my wife and daughters and drive them back to Denver. The exciting thing is that I have now an apartment. It is on 26th and Kipling. "Paramount Manor" is the name of the place. Three bedrooms for $270. It is upstairs. I have a good chance to get one downstairs in a month or so. Last night I went to play bingo, and I won. I interviewed three women for the position of Quality Control Specialist. I still wish you could have applied and probably beaten them to the job. It pays 12 grand plus.

Tomorrow I will probably get up early for the long drive back. It is about 19 hours or so. We are being served a small steak on this flight. It is now 7:30 p.m. and I may miss my connecting flight to El Paso in Albuquerque. I made a football pool for the Super Bowl. The winner will receive two hundred and fifty dollars and the other half of five hundred total goes into the migrant relief fund in the council. Each of the one hundred squares is worth five bucks. Are you a gambler? Would you like for me to pick a square for you and you send me the five dollars later?

Last night I heard a long story about a character who very possibly could have been real. The tale is almost believable. No, Mindy, it is not Bubuluju this time but a woman by the name of Viola Ingersoll. It is more so the story of an integrated barrio in Pueblo, Colorado. As I heard it told it took place some twenty-five years ago, more or less. The young woman who told it to me lived in that barrio. She must have been about six then.

Let me see if I can find the *punta del hilo* of this *relato*. Viola was known to everyone as Vi. There are two versions as to how it came about that she lost her mind. It really does not matter which of the two is true or even if there is a third reason that we do not know anything about. The fact is that she lost her mind . . . *estaba distraida* Vi.

The first reason has it that she had two sons who were but three and five years old respectively. These two boys were playing close to a construction site. They were attracted by the excavation being down where they were to build a smoke stack for the steelmill. Nowadays a highway frames that old neighborhood. This is the setting for the story about Vi and her two boys. While playing they fell into a deep hole dug only a few days earlier and half full of water from a broken main. The two boys drowned.

Vi loved her sons with a few more degrees than it is customary for mothers to love their offspring. This is verified by close acquaintances of Vi who knew her, both before she lost her mental faculties and afterwards. As they tell it she was a very pretty lady, young and neat. Her husband used to manage a department in a big variety store downtown. He made good money for those times and for that particular barrio.

As soon as Vi received the *noticia* that her children were dead, her mind broke like a mirror falling down from the seventh floor of a building. She was immediately hospitalized. Her husband had to tend to the services of the two boys himself.

The other version, and the most credible of the two, is that Vi was driving back from Colorado Springs one time that she had taken them to the zoo. They got caught in a storm. There was an accident and her two boys were killed. She also received a severe head blow and consequently she never regained her full use of reason.

It was not the same after her children were gone. *Los vecinos la consolaban.* Priests and ministers alike tried to explain to her "the will of God" to no avail. Even a couple of sessions with some young psychiatrist from Denver did no good. The choice was very obvious: she had to be institutionalized. Perhaps in a mental institution they could help her. I guess since this is basically a story of extraordinary love we can say that her husband also had that particular kind because he refused to have her committed.

Vi had a distant look in her catlike eyes which mingled yellows, greens and grays so that no one was ever sure what was the actual color of her eyes. Some even claim they were blue. She did not care for her person. She did not care for her house. The contrast was very vivid. People were quick to notice it. She tried to substitute her two lost boys with stray dogs and even with some bought at the pet shop. She had seven dogs in all. She soon became known as the woman of the seven dogs or *la señora de los siete perros*, depending on whether it was *polacos*, chicanos or *italianos* who made comments on her strange behavior.

Among her seven dogs was a Chihuahua pup which no one could tell if it were a pup or a full-grown dog.

The husband at first came from work and tried to tidy up the house and the yard. Soon he knew he could just not keep up. Vi began to accumulate all kinds of toys from Goodwill Industries, from St. Vincent de Paul, The Salvation Army Thrift Store. She would also buy some of the toys at very expensive stores downtown. Her husband began to limit her allowance when he saw how much it was costing him to humor her craziness. After a while he managed all of the money and did not give her any more. He did see that she had enough to eat. Vi also would buy very expensive dresses and coats before her allowance was taken away from her.

She never did wear them, though. She did not take off her faded green long dress and wore her brown coat over it. At the sports shop she had bought two very expensive hammocks which her husband put up for her. One was tied to a tree and to a fence post. The other one was hooked to the yard and a pole of steel which doubled up as a clothesline post.

The husband, because he loved her so much, tolerated her for over six months. One day he did not return from work. Since that one day, no one knew what had happened to him or where he had gone.

Once Vi realized that she had also lost her husband her *locura* grew even more. As her insanity increased so did her popularity with the barrio children. They did not see her as a crazy person. As a matter of fact, they did not see her as anything but saw beyond her into the huge boxes full of toys, which she kept visible in the yard. Vi's *locura* was not of the violent kind. The mothers of the children not only did not prevent the children from visiting her but even encouraged them to do so.

At times as many as twenty children were keeping her company in her yard. The dogs enjoyed the presence of the children also. Vi would just lie in one of the hammocks and read. Her distant look did not leave her eyes even as she read. She would allow the children to play with all the toys. Among the children, and through whose memory this story was transferred to me and to these pages, was that little girl who lived in the neighborhood.

She was, and is, the third born in a family of six. She now has a daughter of her very own. Her daughter is nine years old and she still lives in the same barrio with her grandparents.

Vi had no income. The neighbors took turns seeing that she had at least enough to eat. This is yet another kind of love and concern which is out of the ordinary.

Perhaps Vi would still be living there if it were not for the fact that things did not go well all the time. She had a strange habit of getting up around five a.m. and banging on a cardboard box. Doing this daily she would, in the manner of a rooster, announce the beginning of each new day. She would yell to the entire barrio that it was time to get up. She had a very cute but irritating way of doing it. She would yell at full open-lung volume and repeat the same chant every single day:

—THE MORNING IS COMING.
THE MORNING IS COMING.
RISE TO GREET IT:

RISE TO GREET IT.
RISE UP TO MEET IT.

She would walk up and down the full length of the alley. She was like a drum majorette drumming up on a cardboard box.

Neighbors did anything and everything to make her stop this silly routine. They called the police on her. They threw objects at her. They yelled and cussed at her. Those who spoke English would say,

—All right, all right, you crazy fool. The whole town is up now, thanks to you.

Those who spoke Spanish would join in the commotion to make the whole neighborhood sound like the United Nations,

—Cállese, pinche vieja loca, jija de la chingada.

Some even used their own European languages to make the whole scene even more absurd at that ungodly hour. Some yelled at her in Russian, in Italian or in Polish.

Vi would simply ignore everything and go on about her business of waking up the entire neighborhood. No one could figure out how it was that she would wake up daily with such synchronized precision. She did not have an alarm clock. You could set your watches and clocks by the first pounding on the cardboard box at exactly five a.m.

The neighbors took about as much as they could from Crazy Vi. One Italian woman who lived the furthest away from her initiated a petition to have Vi committed. She had already obtained fifty-two signatures by the time she approached the Chicano household where the little girl lived. The father was quite angry with the Italian lady. He refused to sign the petition. He not only refused to sign it but actually tore it up. The Italian lady had to go home and start a new one all over again. This time she skipped the house of the little girl.

Things did get worse for Vi but not before she had ample time to influence the minds of the little *muchachitos y muchachitas* who were her daily companions. As is recalled and also as it serves to substantiate the old Chicano saying of,

—LOS LOCOS Y LOS BORRACHOS DICEN LA VERDAD.

Vi had the ability to explain highly abstract subjects in such a simple way that even the little children would grasp.

Maybe it was because ever since she had lost her children, time had stopped for her that she would always prefer to talk with them about time and its various dimensions. This would also explain why she would repeat so religiously her five a.m. commotion.

Once as she talked with the barrio children, she got very involved in the idea of eternity. Most of the children thought about eternity as the time between Christmases.

She gathered them around her and told them that she was going to teach them a way of measuring the length, width and size of "ETERNITY." Maybe it was that she herself remembered someone else telling her the story as she herself was a child or maybe she made it up, but this is what she told the children:

—I want you to look at the little girl across the street from us . . .

When she saw that they were able to follow her instructions, she went on.

—Now, do you see that little bird upon that tree branch? I want you to look at it. I want you to look very carefully at that little bird. Do you see how small it is?

The one thing which had not changed about Vi was her pleasant tone of voice. Everything in her life had changed but her melodious soft and sweet voice. The children enjoyed listening to her and her company as well. They loved to hear her stories as they were doing then. Just by luck, a single small bird stood very still on a tree limb. It was winter, that particular time of the year when the branches are bare.

About seven children who listened to this particular verbal illustration of eternity had an ample opportunity to observe the bird which remained almost as if it were a painting or a stuffed one.

Vi continued,

—Now, switch your attention to its wings. Do you see how the wings are made of a few fragile feathers?

As Vi asked this of the children, she reached into her coat pocket and pulled out a small feather. Times like that she appeared to be a teacher with her full use of her faculties who had prepared a lesson extra well. She raised the feather high so as to call attention to the children one degree higher even though all of them were by now hanging onto her every word with their little ears and eyes. The children switched their attention from that little bird, which had not moved an inch, to the feather in Vi's hand. She allowed the children to hold the feather and examine it at close range.

—See how soft and fragile the feather is? Look again at the little bird. Look, it is flying away.

There was an air of excitement in the eyes of the children. There were ooohs and aaahs all around. The bird circled around close by a couple of times and then it disappeared from their view.

—Listen to me, dear children. I want you now to close your eyes and think of a big . . . a very big ball of steel. It is bigger than a marble, bigger than a baseball, bigger than a basketball. The ball of steel is bigger, much bigger, why, it is as big as the whole world. But, of course, you do not know how big this world is, do you? I don't either. You can still go and imagine the biggest ball of steel possible, maybe the size of the moon or the sun, okay?

The children were actually listening very carefully to Vi with their eyes closed. Some had their little hands over their eyes to make sure they were closed. You could tell they were trying very hard to imagine what Vi was asking them to. Some most likely were imagining even more fantastic things with their bright imaginations. How is it that you could tell they were trying is because you could see their young foreheads shaping little black, brown and white frowns.

—That giant ball of steel that you have now fixed in your imagination, I want you to hold if fixed there for a moment. The bird that we just saw fly away is flying close to that ball. it is flying so close that its little wing is brushing against it. The bird is flying clear around the huge ball of steel and brushing it with its wing in one spot only every time it completes one circle. My dear children, when that bird flying around that giant ball of steel manages to wear it out by merely rubbing its little wing in the same spot, then, and only then, will eternity begin.

The children remained very still after Vi stopped talking. They were actually waiting for her to go on with the example, with the little story about the steel ball and the bird. The story did not continue as eternity does. The children were, after all, better off with their own version of what eternity is: that period between Christmases. Vi did not say anything else. She simply ushered the disappointed children out of her yard in the same gentle manner she used with them, touching them very tenderly.

One of the children had kept the feather that Vi had shown them. He pulled a marble out of his jean's pocket and began rubbing the marble with the feather a couple of times. Nothing happened to the marble. He threw the feather away.

Vi must have been a very religious person at one time because a lot of her stories had to do with God. One time she tried to explain to the children the concept of the Blessed Trinity. As with the concept of eternity, she must have failed. It must not have been a total failure, because the young woman recalled it from her childhood. It had stuck in her mind almost word per word.

Vi had a bigger crowd that time. She had sixteen children. Most of them were little girls. One was a young black girl who represented the only black family living in the barrio then. There has not been another black family there since.

This time Vi assumed the role of a nun teaching a class of Catechism.

—There is one God, but that one God is three different persons all at once.

The children had enough of a hard time understanding the idea of one God so that three of them was an overdose of divinity, a divine bureaucracy.

God, the father, created the world. God, the son, saved it from sin, in other words from itself, and God, the Holy Spirit, keeps it running. Much like a car, it is made, it is repaired, and someone drives it.

Vi used to tell these stories from her hammock. Her hands at times would get tangled in the ropes as she gesticulated to illustrate a point.

—All of these three persons in God were, and are, always present in each other. We usually think of them as having happened or happening at different time periods, when actually all of them happen at once. When God the Father created the world, we do not think of Jesus or the Holy Ghost being right there, and then with Him, but they were.

The idea that it was a "him" and not a "her" didn't seem to bother Vi or the children. The one who told me this story went on to become a strong feminist.

—God, the Father, had so much love for what he made that out of his love, a son was created. Out of the love that the Son had for the Father, the Holy Ghost was created.

As Vi said this she gave her word with such a degree of credibility that the children could almost imagine that she had been an eyewitness in all of those magical events. The influence of the Roman Catholic Church in the barrio was strong. It had two churches and one Catholic school. The school and one of the two churches is gone now, but one church remains.

Because of this influence, the children had a vivid image in their minds of what Jesus Christ looked like. The few pictures in their *catecismos* made God, the Father, look like Jesus, only older with puffy cheeks. As far as they could tell, both of them were human beings like their *tíos* and *abuelitos*.

—I know you cannot picture the idea of the Holy Ghost or of the three persons who are in God, or what it looks like to have two of them coming out of the one. I cannot help much in making you understand this. Listen, children, close your eyes and see if you can bring to your minds the big lake at the north side of the city.

Vi had to do this using first a lake as an example, as she knew none of the children had ever seen the sea. The lake in the north side was not big at all. It was man-made, but most of the children had been there on picnics with their parents.

—Make believe, children, that the lake is bigger, much bigger than the whole state, even bigger than the country. Can you imagine how much water it would hold? It is millions of times greater than if we were to fill up all of the bathtubs of the world or if we were to open all of the faucets of the world and let them run for a whole year. It is as if we were to have rain come to us for a whole month at a time.

The children got a good idea of what amount of water she was talking about. She went into the house without saying why. She came back with a toy shovel and a tiny bucket. She also had a shoebox full of sand. All of the children gathered closer to see what she was going to do with these items. They anticipated they were going to participate in an experiment of some sort. They thought and knew that whatever those items were they were part of her story.

—I want you to see the lake again with your minds. Now I want you to imagine yourselves getting all the water from the lake and pouring it in this little hole I have made in the sand. That is what the little bucket is for, for you to bring all of that water and pour it in the sandbox.

The black girl spoke up.

—Oh, Vi, you're silly. We can't do that. We need a bigger bucket and a bigger shoebox.

—Exactly, Vi cut in—. You cannot do that. The idea of the blessed Trinity is the water and the shoebox is our head.

We cannot fit such a big idea into our heads, they are too small.

As Vi thought she had finally succeeded in getting her point across, two of her seven dogs began fighting with each other. All of the attention was switched to the dogfight. A little girl started to hit one of the dogs with the bucket, while a boy dumped the sand in the shoebox on top of the other. They were all trying in one way or another to keep the dogs from fighting.

The barrio was much more than Vi. Vi was never actually put away in the nuthouse in the San Luis Valley even though the efforts to do so by some of the neighbors did continue. She died. For the first time in over one year and one half, the sound of the cardboard box being banged by her at exactly five a.m. was not heard. Rain or snow, she would greet each morning the same way.

Some swear, and that is what's so strange about her story, that she actually never had a husband or children. Her reality was our fantasy, our fantasies about her reality.

The story of this barrio in Pueblo, Colorado, is as the soap operas shown on TV every day. It changes and it grows. It ends and it begins.

There was the Russian lady who lived three houses down from the Chicano family to whom the little girl belonged. She had as much trouble with the English language as most Chicanos had.

—Goot, girl . . . Goot, children . . . nice . . . very nice, children, she would say to the mothers who on Sundays used to display their children in the best attire, as they went to church.

This story is about unusual love . . . or the lack of it. In the barrio also lived a woman who had a little girl. I do not remember her name. She used to tend bar downtown in order to support that one child. She had no husband. She had to leave the girl by herself in the house. She was but five. All of the neighbors worried about the little girl. They would make the *mala cara* when they saw the woman. This was a sign of disapproval with her job and with leaving the girl alone. They would meet her on her way to get *pan y leche* and would not give her the *buenos días.*

There was a Chicano family also with seven brothers. They were as mean as you can imagine. Few dared to tangle with any of them for fear of arousing the other six. They used to beat up on some intruders into the barrio. The good thing about them, as the little girl remembers, was that they never did beat up anyone who was a *conocido.* As if their mean ways were not enough, they also had three vicious big dogs which, even though they were hardly needed, were highly considered whenever anyone decided to get into a hassle with them.

A young teenager lived in the barrio with his grandmother. They were hillbillies. He was both hated and pitied by the barrio people. His name was Tom. He had already been an alcoholic for three years even though he was no more than sixteen. He would come home drunk. This would be in the early mornings, long before Vi would get up to bang on the cardboard box. He would be all *borracho,* and would knock on the door trying to get his grandmother to open up the door. The grandmother was hard of hearing so he would soon resort to kicking the door open.

—Open up, gran'maw, it's me, Tom.

Open this Goddamn door now.

It's very cold out here . . . hurry up, gran'maw.

The old *viejita* looked weak and sick. Tom was known to knock her around a bit along with the furniture after he got in the house. The commotions were frequent. There was a lot of cussing on Tom's part and the breaking of dishes and throwing around of chairs.

The *abuelita* finally died. Tom went away.

Yes, the barrio is still there. The problems are new. I am sure there is a new Tom and a new Vi. Some are finding out about drugs while others are finding out about Jesus. They try to hang on to either as if they were drowning and Jesus and the drugs were liferafts.

There is the family man who fell in love with a younger woman and gave her love and money. There is the man who does not know how to cope with the situation of loving a wife so much and getting zero return for his investment.

There are times when the joy of living is polluted by situations beyond all possible control. Undesired situations which must be borne.

There are new generations ready to bury the old ones and create those of the next century. There is a man watching TV and reading the newspaper. Once in a while he allows a thought about his first wife to enter his cluttered mind. Once in a while he remembers the days of the pachucos and how he used to chase a few skirts in those days . . . and catch them.

People can live in a barrio and very little difference does it make in the long run what nationality they are. There are the same ingredients present. There is an abundance of cruelty among that poverty. There is the wife who hates the husband, and most likely spits on his breakfast and cusses at him under her breath for fear of being heard. There is the husband who, in a drunken stupor, goes on to abuse his wife and children. Paradoxically, he beats them up to earn their respect.

The teller of these tales just drove to that fictitious barrio in that fictitious town of Pueblo, Colorado. I received a Christmas card from her today. The card had a beautiful picture of a bird. The bird was much like the one which rubs his wing against the huge steel ball called eternity. Actually, when that wing manages to wear out that ball, eternity will only be beginning.

She had written me a letter before. She never did get around to sending it to me until she had written a second letter, and then she included both of them. One was a happy, sharing letter, while the other although being very honest, did not stop from being a sad Dear John type of letter. She gets angry at me because I tend to laugh at what she considers very serious things, but she remembers I cry at silly movies.

It is a good thing that the woman I am speaking about is also a fictitious character or else I think I could have become very easily the third man who loves her very much and spoils her a great deal.

I had bought her a pair of brown earrings the color of her eyes, and she had promised to make me a coffee mug in her ceramics class. Just because both of us are not real, there is no reason for the gifts, which are real, not to be exchanged.

I choose to close these *cuentos* with one which is yet the warmest of them all—a mother-daughter love *cuento* which also belongs in that mythical barrio in Pueblo.

It seems that the nine- or ten-year-old girl with the royal name, and her mother with the goddess of peace name, await until moments just before Christmas or New Year, and very quietly and casually sneak out of the house where other people are and go on for a long long walk by themselves, arm in arm. They walk together the streets of that barrio where once the mother was a little girl. Among many caresses and tender touches, they share very quiet moments just walking. They greet those holidays in like fashion as if saying to them and to the world that they can take on whatever life dishes their way . . . together. The father of that little girl probably imagines their walk from his lonely cell in Canyon City Prison.

Some of us live such a fantastic reality that we are shocked when others refer to it as a mere fantasy.

Some of us have no business at all mingling with normal people because our continuous strokes of insanity are indeed hard to take or comprehend. One moment we are praising God for his creation and the next moment we wish that a semi would run us over.

Some of us escape a few nights from our daily routines. We are frightened by the overwhelming reality around us. We rent a room in the first motel we see and go on to make love. We whisper love words and agonizing angry words to each other for the duration of that one night. We express our doubts with eloquence and mumble our credos.

Some of us refuse with all our strength to stop the whirl of activity. We pray to God for more phone calls, for more letters, for more meetings, for more involvement, for more commitments, for more work, so that at no time we find ourselves alone, and thus have to face ourselves.

The one who told me these tales says she no longer fears herself. Now she loves herself. She enjoys her own company very much. At times she spends even two or three whole days by herself drinking hot tea and looking out the window.

I only wish I were a Cervantes or a Shakespeare to take these inanimate characters and blow life into them with my red ballpoint pen or kiss them tenderly on their eyes or necks so that they would escape the deathspell and would gather life. I only wish . . .

Dearest Mindy, you must excuse this lengthy letter. I just couldn't stop. At times, I swear to you, I saw myself in the words I was printing on the paper. I lost all track or length of time. I actually felt myself cold and alone in that integrated barrio. I kept waiting for Vi to bang on her cardboard box and wake me up. She never did. I kept listening for that drunk teenager to call on his grandmaw, but the— Open up, gran'maw . . . —never reached my ears. Once I even turned around to see if anyone was really taking toy bucketfuls of water from the sea and emptying them in the shoebox full of sand, but all I saw around me were walls, cars driving by, people I did not know.

Mindy, after a lengthy bout like this one, I am completely exhausted in my mind. I reach for a beer and the latest copy of *Mad* magazine.

This barrio assumes certain human characteristics which sociologists go on to illustrate in textbooks as caricatures. Assuming a human form also means that the barrio develops a philosophy of life. It knows it must sustain itself by whatever means or hustles possible. It must manufacture its own pride out of the raw materials there. The barrio knows the skin of its streets and alleys trap people within . . . but also keeps those from without. Barrios fight the bulldozer and the ironball of progress which is bent on destroying them and turning them into warehouses and freeways.

Most of us who grew up in a barrio miss the heartbeat of that body. We now go on as individual cells seeking a new body. Suburbia is a rather poor substitute, the skeleton is most of the times full of decay. The campus does not come close to the vibrant torso of society: THE BARRIO.

Denver's West Side, El Paso's El Segundo, East Los have a very definite pulse and smell. Albuquerque, Laredo, Phoenix, Chicago, Oakland, San Antonio and all of the Harlems of the world are all *cunas* of pride and the best of settings for the human tragedy and comedy of life.

Through the broken windows of the minds of two individuals you have looked into one such barrio, Mindy. The Eternal Bill Collector, the Eternal Social Worker seems to visit our barrios constantly looking for all of his lost *borreguitos*.

LA LLORONA: An Epic Poem
(1980)

La Llorona

la llorona . . . the wailing one
keeps crying for her lost son.
in each culture,
in each religion,
in each country,
in each city
there is a legend
of *la llorona.*
nature intended
for grandfathers to die first
and then their parents
and then the children
        and grandchildren.
when the process is reversed
nature itself
        pierces the heavens
with cries of anguish.
. . . in her own language.
la llorona . . . the wailing one
keeps crying for her lost son.
when cortés
conquered the aztecs
in tenochtitlán
        he took
a beautiful aztec woman,
la malinche,
and they had a son,
one of the first mestizos,
one of the first chicanos.
when the child grew up
cortés wanted to send him to europe
to be educated
as an *español* . . . as a white man.
la malinche, rather than giving

her son to such a fate,
went to a high cliff to cast him down.
la llorona . . . the wailing one
keeps crying for her lost son.
tenochtitlán
is now mexico city
and many are those who swear
that in the dead of night
when the wind blows cold
la malinche, symbol of all mothers
in the world,
gives out her painful cries.
her crying
                is more than sorrowful lament
and regret,
it is a warning
to protect the descendants
of the aztecs
from the dangers
of materialism.
la llorona . . . the wailing one
keeps crying for her lost son.
in the dark hall
of a high school
in rocky ford, colorado,
when it would get dark
many students of that time,
when the somber arch entrance
was still standing,
recall *la llorona* and shiver
as she would break out
her deafening wail.
could it be
she suffers still
the bad education
chicanitos are receiving
all over the country . . .

could it be?
la llorona . . . the wailing one
keeps crying for her lost son.
in trinidad, colorado,
a mother lost her little boy.
he was run over
                by a train.
even today trains are known
to slam the breaks
when upon the same spot
they hear the cry of the mother
break their eardrums.
in la junta, colorado,
by the arroyo
where a young girl
committed suicide
and a little boy
fell facedown on the mud of the arroyo
la llorona . . . the wailing one
keeps crying for her lost son.
alurista, the poet, writes,
"she cries *en las barrancas* of industry
her children devoured by computers,"
the virgin mary cries for her son on the cross.
ay, ¿dónde está mi hijo?
ay, ay, mis hijos queridos.
ay, ay, ay, i want my children.
ay, ay, ay, ay, se murió mi hijo.
then there is a long silence
louder than her cry
and the goose bumps multiply.
ay, ay, ay, ay, ay . . . .
la llorona . . . the wailing one
keeps crying for her lost son.

Captando el Cuarto Canto

if we could bottle the *optimismo*
de torero este canto no sería el mismo.
if only we could borrow
a bit of his wisdom
la raza would invite
trabajadores culturales
to their own *canto*
instead of the other way around.
el cuarto canto,
                        despite shortcomings,
está a toda.
it elevates
to an indigenous
spiritual level
missing in the other three.
but . . .
no te agüites,
as long as there is life
there are a hell of a lot of "buts"
to be expected.
pero . . .
sí, la raza
ya ha progresado mucho.
ya mero llega
al bendito pinche
que la parió.
pinche used here
metaphorically
meaning the door
which gave us
our existence.
el vento *y el* lalo
y los dos joses
se miraban uno al otro.

in the ten-day duration
of *el festival en* mesa, arizona,
and *lugares circumvecinos*
the *canto* is bound to have
many miracles
including rain
during the greeting of the sun
ceremony monday morning.
it would have come out a lot better
if many other *carnales*,
including those with resources,
had thrown their support this way
but then again
si mi tía tuviera ruedas
fuera bicicleta
y la política local
constipa a la estatal
y la estatal a la nacional
y así es por los siglos
de los siglos amén.
la emy *y* burciaga
se agüitan pero no cuitean
y se van con los campesions
a darle gas
y compartir el arte con ellos
que por cualquier
otro nombre

                          se conoce como corazón.
ahí van llegando otros de austin
arrestaron a dos en el chuco.
la carnala de sanjo

                          loves to paint
but cannot find the time to do it
since she has to raise a *familia*
and so *le echa brochazos*
ya late when all have gone to bed.
besides she has to double as

a bread-winner to help the husband
make the payments and the bills.
una carnala de michigan
carga sus cinco cuadros.
los indios de mejicles
y los de canadá
y los carnales de el salvador
y uno de sweden *platican*
sin entenderse.
you can chalk it off
as *pura destrampología,*
misguided *energía,*
a strong case *of yo-no-sabía*
o que el quinto sol

> *se moría.*

we are clean people. *en medio de todo*
nos sacudimos el lodo.

Vo

el niño no tiene cuna.
los gatos arañan la luna
panza arriba en la azotea.
en el panteón rechinan las cajas de los muertos
mientras que unos lagartijos tuertos
azotan sus lenguas largas
contra un jamoncillo rancio.
lo cierto es
                que ya es el tiempo
de experienciar
visiones apocalípticas
                      y ver las mentiras claras
sin el uso de telescopios.
yo pensé
              que unos indios
                    bien empeyotados
le cantaban a la oscuridad
salpicando agua bendita
sobre una computadora nueva
pero me fijé más de cerca
y vi que eran unos científicos
contando granos de arena
sobre una ballena
envenenada en la playa.
busqué el sol
en el dedo gordo.
no lo encountré
pero me quemé.

147

Space Age

volando va el viejo sueco
con alas de garabato chueco.
viste de piel de rana africana,
empuña una verde macana
y por la ventana
                    de su cohete
a propulsión molcajete
se asoma y ve a la luna
hacerle esquina a la bruma.
va a apadrinar matrimonio
tres estrellas y cuatro cometas
más delante.
el sol tamaño elefante
quema metales de aguante
más el de adobe
                    y la quijada
como un compás.
lo de ser sueco es un disfraz,
en verdad es un azteca,
no, es un indio huichol
orutando leche, petróleo y alcohol,
rayándole la madre al sol
y al dios bizco explotador
que inventó el disco volador.

De Frisco a Boise

—sir, what would you like to drink?

sangre.
la sangre tibia de mártires antiguos
piped to my lips by huesos consagrados.
agua.
agua helada destilada en pilas
colocadas en las cinco esquinas del infierno
para tentar almas eternamente condenadas.
leche.
leche humana de unos pechos negros
hinchados con el amor enpedernido
de mil amantes separados.
miel.
the honey of two million bees
dripping a new sex life to a cock
dead for five centuries
which has turned into two dozen rusty worms.
wine.
el vino olvidado en la bodega
hecho de cinco mil uvas asoleadas
para celebrar una boda conmigo mismo.
atole.
atole champurrado hecho por ocho abuelas
meneado con sus dedos ampollados
y endulzado con sus sonrisas arrugadas
y un pedazo de piloncillo verde.
pink champagne.
champaña rosa para hacer un último brindis
a un camino . . . a un volcán . . . a un maguey.

—sir, why do you ask for such odd things?
because my thirst is that of tres pobres peones
and four aztec kings.

Shssst

shsst . . . calla.
no es tu culpa. fue el canalla.
el canalla del destino.
temía yo
que llegara tal momento
en el cual mi contento
se volviera limonada
y el amor nada,
el mismo amor que en un día atrás
formara montañas
verdes de calor.
shsssst, calla.
la batalla
           ni siquiera comenzó
sin embargo
ya se considera terminada,
ganada
           y perdida.
qué sabes tú de sacrificio.
aún tu muela del juicio
viaja en cápsulas
           por el espacio.
eres joven
y un viejo zorro
como yo
      no tiene ningun derecho
de inflamar tu pecho
con fantasías
de la grandeza
empapadas en un mar de ternura.
a la mejor nos perdemos en la playa.
shsssst . . . calla.

Metz

—A company that earns one dollar a share and writes off three
dollars a share in depreciation expense actually generates four
dollars in cash.

Stock Market Detective Work
Robert Metz

is the origin of capitalism
in the premordial baptism
of creation,
inflation
      in the first human seed?
weeds used as coins
to buy the cosmic dust
of two billion years ago.
how much is each share worth now
on a cow,
       a worm,
            a flower?
i send my granddaughter, Amanda,
ten bucks a month.
they are my ten bucks
and i can do with them
whatever i wish
but what about the time
when she is twenty-one
and she has all these dollars
in her hand or in the bank?
what will the *centenares* of amandas
from south america, africa
y américa misma
think of her? of me?
should I stop sending her ten bucks?
what of the right to private property . . . to accumulate,
the right to exploit and speculate.

Living Life on His Own Terms
(2001)

More than fifty years ago,

I discovered that I enjoy writing. It has been a love affair ever since. I confess that I may not be too good at it but it matters little because the fact is, I enjoy writing.

The Xicano Movement came along in the sixties and gave me a great boost. I began to chronicle events and create a lasting logo of all our glory and suffering. I also found myself using what I wrote as a way of inspiring those in the struggle. I may even have inspired others to write and create their art. I know for a fact I was one of those who pioneered hard for our Xicano literature to become part of American literature.

Recently I have been receiving all kinds of recognition for my literary efforts, humble that they may be. I even had the opportunity to represent my country in Valencia, Spain, at a world conference on literature.

Time has caught up with me and I see the golden years engulf me and it makes me very sad that I am not the fifteen-year-old boy in South El Paso, the first one in the barrio to buy an Underwood typewriter, *en abonos*, to type my first poems and *cuentos*.

It has been a wonderful journey and I feel it will continue yet for some time to be so. These writings may very well by my second literary wind and the best I have to write may remain the same . . . to make the reader think. To make all readers discover their beauty and wonder hiding just under their skins, their many shades of skin.

The unexplainable urge to share my thoughts is young in contrast to my gray hair and aging muscles. In such spirit, I share these verses, these poems, these pages . . .

Living Life on His Own Terms

I think of my son Abelardo Delgado
whimsically as a combination of
Tom Sawyer and Atilla the Hun
and that's quite a combination.
Certainly he has the boyishness,
the honesty, humor capacity
for adventure and zest for life of a Sawyer.

Well, I must say he is one of today's greats.
One of those rare ones who might just
sum up the spirit of the times.
So far as his own life is
concerned he comes out fighting.
Let's face it, he says it in his intensely
dark eyes, if you want to get anything
done in this down to earth world
you've got to fight.
it's just one big battle by all means.

He works things out this way.
If he doesn't like something, he just don't do it.
This has meant some mightly tussels
before he's been able to buy his
own ticket and do what he's wanted to do.
However, Lalo's enthusiasm is contagious.

I must say, when friends approach him
he goads and tempts and bugs and dares
you into ventures and adventures you
would normally not dream of
undertaking, that only an adolescent
or testing to be sure the cool is there.
Well . . . it still is.

Like Tom Sawyer, he wants to try everything,
wants to live dangerously, accept the risks that
float down that river on a homemade raft,
like Atilla, once he's on the raft it becomes
a galleon of war. He becomes a strong man others
tremble at the sound of his voice.

Yet Lalo finds
success a little difficult—it includes the
gladhand bit which he hates
a lot of activities he labels phony
a lot more work that he wants to do and a threat
to his deeply personal life.
No one but no one is going to
tell him how to live. A pro would undertake,
on horse racing, cars, dogs, this is the constant
text, always, he is testing.

He follows his instincts and so far so good,
but it's not easy, it can only be done by fighting
for your own identity, closing the door
on your private life and keeping your cool.
In this Corner at 210 pounds wearing a mustache
and his own fierce ideals.

ABELARDO DELGADO

He is the man power—the strength of the
King of the Huns.

By his mother
Mrs. Guadalupe B. Díaz Delgado
Guadalupe B. Díaz passed away March 5, 2000.

Bring in the Lions

The leprosy of our days
is to have contracted AIDS.
Rhyan White succumbs at eighteen,
we shed a crocodile tear,
still prevailing is the fear.

Prejudicial ignorance
remains from biblical times.

We still fear God's hand
for things we don't understand,
we still build city islands
to outcast the scarlet A's
but we're now
entering
the new age of
compassion,
Easters of understanding
will prevent us from driving
nails of shame through fragile hands
of those already dying.

Come on, bring in the lions,
come on, burn them at the stake,
stone them with indifference
and hang bells around their necks.

No, we haven't learned anything,
we are still back at the jungle
and ignorance is the king.

The Holy Dove lost a wing
changing overreactions
into needed actions.

Yes, we can embrace a man
with AIDS without fear
of him contaminating
that embrace and kiss a child
with *SIDA* preserving yet
the innocence of such a kiss. Those with AIDS are not IMMUNE
to hate and in their tender hearts
there is no love DEFICIENCY.

The SYNDROME is unconcern
ACQUIRED throughout the ages.

He would be found among them
if Christ were here today
and He would do more than pray.

Dallas/Ft. Worth to Denver

Do not ask, I don't know why
but I'm not afraid to die,
I'm much more afraid of living.

Alive I'm forced to be a witness
to all crimes,
committed now
and in times past.

Alive I must bear the pain,
shout and complain each
inhumanity,
each effervescent lie.

No, I'm not afraid to die,
it is my life
that scares me
half to death

Each doubt I have
is already my coffin
and each
dishonest
hand I shake
is a cold deserted cemetery.

I carry death's welcome mat
in my back pocket
wherever I go.

Death can come
whenever it wants to.

No, I am not afraid to die,
however, living
brings me a chilling panic.

The quadraphonic silence
fits the nakedness
of my existence
and constantly reminds me
of the distance
between the purpose of my life
and my actions.

No, I'm not afraid to die,
what's more
I think I've done it once before.
Death can suck at my last hard-on
before it is gone.

Harmony in Diversity

A one-letter alphabet
is one we would not forget
   . . . or use.
A one-word dictionary
is a bit extraordinary
but of no use.
In Arizona or New Mexico
in a clear midnight
go out and see
if you can see
only one star.
For long in the U.S.
we have known
a university
was not an Angloversity.
A single musical note
is not a symphony
and a violin is just fine
until joined by another 99
and the rhapsody floods the ear.
Yes, even God
who is said to but one
decided to multiply Himself
into the Blessed Trinity.
Diversity is not right or wrong,
diversity just is.
Imagine the human body
all eyes, noses or ears
or worse yet butts.
Imagine the frustration
if you bought a lotto quickpick
and got the same numbers
everyone else did.
What would the FBI do

if all the fingerprints
were alike?
Think of today's Babylonians
advocating English only,
 . . . whites only,
that could turn out
quite lonely.
There is harmony in diversity
and not any controversy.

Mind Wonderings

Close your eyes and see beyond
the world of which we're so fond.

Pierce the universe
with your imagination
and see if you can find
an end to God's creation.

No wonder
some deny God
for they think,
and think it odd,
that if there is a god
He or she would bother
to be of this grain of sand
called man
a father . . . or mother.

Without God man is
supreme
but sadly only a dream
because dreams are
measured
in minutes and in hours,
no matter how powerful,
this life of ours.

So God created, so what?
All was left in time to rot,
think some of us
with cloudy minds,
as man's mind be,
but fail to see
God creates continuously.

There's no greater fool
than he
who says limited can be
the things that God can do.

The fool does that
because his mind
cannot run those things.
The relationship
between God
and man is faith, or sin,
a faith to accept God is one
who values souls more than the sun.

My Mother, Part I

My mother, the phoenix
flying over tall trees,
rising from the ashes,
flying Heaven bound,
caught by Heaven's Hound,
my mother the phoenix.

My mother did not die
last Sunday morning
but when she lost her independence,
when she stopped being self-sufficient,
my mother, the strong woman.

Silently she explains her own death,
one last breath,
a diminishing heartbeat,
tired, winding down.

Her death is a question mark,
an exclamation point,
a period to end
the story of her life
or just a comma
promising that there is more.

My mother, the teacher
who taught me to love life,
to enjoy it,
to get up after every tumble
to end the race, the task, proud, humble.

My Mother, Part II

My mother, the miracle,
to the end always on call,
who by generic magic
has lost her shell
but not her spirit.

She now constantly breathes
through the young lungs
of her young grandchildren,
whose heart still beats
through their strong beats.

My mother, the dancer
who enjoyed music
and a well-waxed dance floor,
who erred much
but was forgiven
because she also loved much.

All good-byes are painful
but the most painful of all
is the one said
by a departing soul
which leaves those behind,
confused, mute, blind,
in the midst of blends
of unexplainable sadness
and happiness like lulling rain,
mere so-long 'til we meet again.

I don't feel right,
I feel like a kite,
which has lost its string.

I'm wrong, the string is still there
pulling, guiding from above.

My mom, who used to say
we should be grieving for the living
for all the dead rejoice
listening to God's voice.

A Word

A word is a musical note
wearing t-shirt or tie and coat.

A word is a musical note,
a teacher or a silly goat.

A word is a musical note,
a candidate getting one vote.

A word is a musical note
eating fries with a root-beer float.

A word is a musical note,
just a footnote, a silly quote.

A word is a musical note
that's riding in a parade float.

A word is a musical note
a bridge over the castle's moat.

It's a Flip of the Coin

The new age of compassion
predicated by thinkers in our nation
started out with a bang,
a lot of bangs in Baghdad.

Newsweek, on the other hand,
says we are reentering
the age of anxiety,
an age in which our society
feels at home,
at ease.

It seems that anxiety,
being an intrinsic part
of our status quo
provides us with tranquility
while compassion,
the new experience,
awakens in us
the primitive fear of the unknown.
Flip a coin to see who won.

Penitente

He's hallowed clay
with both feet
on the ground.

He's got two strikes
against him
but he'll go down swinging.

He has so much good to say
but he's always found full of
dislikes.

He's lemonade
on a mystic
river
flowing streamup.

He's on a masquerade
disguised as a wide receiver
with a tin cup.

Sabastian Michael

Sebi, the baby boy,
anticipating joy,
came during the first Lent
in the first millennium

Sabastian Michael
came just in time to bridge
winter with spring,
Pisces with Aries.

The virgin Mary herself
came down from heaven
to help the doctor
bring him into the world

Now he just eats and sleeps
but surely he is dreaming
of the many things he'll do
as an angel in the crew.

Where?

Where is the voice
I love to hear?

Muffled in a silent tear.

Where are the eyes
I love to see?

Behind those mountains
which grow no tree.

Where are the lips
I love to kiss?

Sealing an
envelope
which brings me
peace.

Where is the hand
I love to touch?

Writing   a   letter   I   need   so   much.

At Socorro High

At Socorro High
there's a lot of pride
because here teachers
help students prepare
to improve, to change
the future of their communities,
their state
their nation
and ultimately the world.

With young dark eyes
they'll light up the darkness
of the new millennium,
with bright creative minds
they'll add that needed magic
to dull, lifeless technology.

I see these bulldogs,
eager, restless
spirits anchored to their desks
like rockets
awaiting launch-off.

I see a brotherhood yet unknown
of Anglos, Xicanos, Indians, Asians
and Blacks, caring for each other
much like a true sister and brother.

Carta Abierta a España

Un candente verano
vino un xicano
a saludar a los abuelos,
veradaderos, míticos,
fantasmas con cascos
de conquista
que le dieron
vida el mestizo,
al mexicano
ya más delante
al llamado xicano.

Estos españoles
aunque no fueran
abuelos invitados
no dejan de ser abuelos.

Por ellos el xicano
carga una religión
muy roja en sus venas
y ya no habla en náhuatl,
ahora periquea en caló
y no le reza al sol,
hoy le reza a Cristo y a María.

Todo esto parece ser
una pesadilla histórica
donde el dolor y la gloria
bailan al son de la realidad.

Qué, España
os debemos la existencia
y heredados están
los dones españoles

de orgullo y de soberbia.
Oh, España
que los xicanos

quisieran negar el parecido
basta con un espejo
para que refleje lo que es
y lo que ha sido.

Un Xicano vino a Valencia
y se quedó sorprendido
de ver que ahí
como en Mexico,
como en los Estados Unidos,
también es su casa,
también es su casa.

El Río Grande I

Jorobado y arrugado
como viejo mal cuidado
va mi Río Grande
ya menos apurado,
con el soquete del tiempo manchado,
por dos países maltratado.

Si en vez de crujir
tus aguas
platicaran
qué de hazañas nos
contaran.

y si tus granos
de arena miraran
cuánta mentira con su mirar
nos desataran.

Tú has visto sufrir al mejícano
cambiar su sudor
por tus aguas mano a mano.

Tú le has dado a la lechuga
el chile como hermano
y al tomate
lo cambiaste en algo humano.

En ancas de una mula
cuando niño te crucé.

Miras tú el contrabando
que el de la aduana
no ve
sirves de espejo

a la esperanza que se fue
y vives esperando la lluvia
que una negra nube dé.

Río Grande, Río Bravo,
polvo de Texas,
ramas de Nuevo Mexico,

ranas de California
y saguaros de Arizona
en conjunto te dan serenata.

Para los enamorados
tus orillas son mil camas
que ellos usan.

Río Grande, ya tienes canas
son unos carrizos amarillos,
la migra disfrazada de grillos.

El Río Grande II

Río Grande, tu fama es mundial
y tiene un lugar muy especial
en dos países
que mucho se odian
que poco se quieren,
que viven como dos malos vecinos.

Río Grande, en veces
tus aguas se tiñen
con la sangre de un
c o n t r a b a n d i s t a
y se aluzan como si fuera
a salir al foro
un gran actor
pero sólo es un
r e f l e c t o r
que ayuda a la migra
a atrapar otro indocumentado
que esa noche se jugó su suerte.

Río Grande, tú eres
tú eres
la puerta más dura
tu separas al hombre
y haces de sus sueños
y ambición basura.

A menudo se lee
que se ahogó
otro mexicano
que te quizo cruzar
sin tener papeles.

Él venía a los estados unidos
a buscar fortuna, y en tus aguas
su muerte fue a encontrar.

Río Grande, un día
no muy lejano
las fronteras se van a acabar
así que habla pronto,
Río Grande, que el tiempo
te va matar.

Cien kilos de yerba
y muchos más de cocaína
vienen envueltos en tus sombras
tú, calmado, no te asombras.

Madre

Madre es la palabra
pa' que el cielo se abra.

Madre lo dice todo
y lo que la misma vida
lleva como apodo.

Madre es la mitad
de mi cuerpo
que al cielo camina.

Madre es la tierna mano
que toca mi frente
y un buen ejemplo de lo que es
        decente.

Madre es la cadena antigua
que nos trajo a todos
y madre es la señora
de los buenos modos.

Por las venas de una madre
corre un amor muy rojo
y aún hay sonrisa en su mueca
cuando enseña enojo.

En su pelo blanco
ya un libro se ha escrito
y cada que ella sufre
la falta de un hijo
el cielo da un grito.

Ella es el bocado de sustento
que a los hijos da aliento
y la oración sincera

que desparrama el viento.
Su mirada es tierna
cual paloma herida
y su vientre un dulce costal
que produce vida.

Su palabra es vara
que indica buena vereda
y su consejo
lo que el hijo hereda.

Ella es una manta blanda
a sus hijos protegiendo,
de los males escondiendo.

¿Por Qué?

¿Por qué rosas?
Son hermosas
y huelen bien lindo
y son símbolos
de vidas breves
pero muy alegres.

¿Por qué rosas?
Porque son las flores
que la Madre de Dios escogió
para pintarse a sí misma.

¿Por qué rosas?
Porque tienen espinas
y ellas representan
el dolor
que la vida carga
entre lo bonito
y las espinas también son
los misterios dolorosos
del rosario
que a la Virgen
le gusta que recemos.

¿Por qué rosas?
Porque las rosas nacen
como nació el Niño Dios
que vino a alegrar y a salvar al mundo,
a saludar al sol
como lo hacían los indios aztecas.

¿Por qué rosas?
Porque son color de la sangre
que en la cruz derramó Cristo,

rojas, blancas y amarillas
como los cielos cambiaron de color
al verlo morir.

¿Por qué rosas?
Fíjese, así son las cosas,
La Madre María de Guadalupe
escogió rosas de invierno
para dejarnos su cara morena,
su cuerpo entero, en la tilma
que el indio Juan Diego llevaba
aquel doce de diciembre de 1531.

¿Por qué no mariposas
en lugar de la rosas?

Qué Bochorno

Qué bochorno tener que morir,
tener que dejar de sentir,
tener que irse lejos de todos
sin poder volver
a verlos jamás.

Ricardo Sánchez muere
pero no sin usar
su misma muerte
como una última lección
como lo hizo Jesucristo.

Decía el,
—Hay que vivir
con dignidad
y hay que festejar la vida
aún el día
que trae la muerte.

Con qué valentía pelea Sánchez
contra el cáncer,
se prendía con sus uñas
de la vida,
peleando por un último suspiro.

Este escritor será
recordado y honrado
por sus creaciones literarias
pero otros preferimos
recordarlo por sus hechos,
por su firmeza,
por su mirada encendida,
siempre retando, interrogando
a falsos profetas
y poetas.

Este Sánchez
nos abandonó una manaña,
un domingo,
el 3 de septiembre del 95
porque el tigre y José Montalvo
tenían un Flor y Canto
en el cielo
con santos y ángeles
y lo invitaron a compartir
sus versos que no saben morir.

Qué bochorno tener que morir,
qué bochorno tenerse que ir.

Cabezón

Decían los que lo conocían
que él era un cabezón
y con el corazón
pensaba en vez de la cabeza.

Era muy testarudo
y siempre sin razón
siempre un cabezón.

Sucedió que un día
oía una canción,
con mucha ilusión
se enamoró de la tristeza.

Va usted a saber
que dio tal tropezón
el viejo cabezón.

Encontró una novia
y perdió la razón
el viejo cabezón
al beber chorros de su belleza.

Ahora él es calmado
y no es cabezón
perdió el corazón.

Café con Besos

Invierno o verano,
tarde o temprano,
me gusta el café con besos.

Me tiembla la mano,
salta el gusano
mientras endulzo mi café
con el azúcar de tus besos.

Se escucha un piano
y el aeroplano
de tu cuerpo
me lleva en un vuelo de esos
en que el café se toma caliente.

Café valenciano
o café cubano
con besos saben igual.

El negro, el hispano
y el americano
toman taza tras taza
calentando todos sus huesos.

Resulta en vano
estar malo o sano
si le faltan besos a mi café,
discafeinados o espressos
son más sabrosos diente con diente.

Calaveras

Volaban las banderas
luciendo calaveras
mientras los esqueletos
marchaban de dos en dos.

Ya tenían ojeras,
sus ojos como peras
que como tantos amuletos
les daba santa claus
en cada Navidad.

Sobraban las calaveras
como si fueran calabazas,
ojos iluminados
como ojos de pescados
después de morder el anzuelo.

Ya no tenían caderas
pero bailaban muy bien
al son de obligados
porque son mal pagados
por las pobres calaveras.

Él

Él se fue
yo quedé
a esperar mi turno.

Desperté
encontré
que en un momento mágico
su espíritu
habia dejado el cascarón
para que lo echaran al cajón.

Yo lloré
yo pensé
que siempre tendría padre.

Yo no sé
si se fue
derecho al cielo
o paró en algún lugar
a escuchar aquella canción
o para coger el mismo camión.

El Araña

En una montaña en España
hay una muy pequeña cabaña
donde vive el araña

El araña come caña
y teje su telaraña
sobre una cizaña

De pronto viene una alimaña
muy apestosa
    porque no se baña
y quiere comerse al araña.

El alimaña le cierra un ojo
y se desbaraña una pestaña
limpiándose una lagaña.

Dice el araña
        —Ésta está muy extraña
        y a mí no me engaña.

el araña saca maña
de su entraña
y usa su telaraña
como una trampolina diciendo,
        —Salto fuera del alcance
        del alimaña
        si no me daña.

Ésta es la hazaña del araña
que también come mucha lasaña.

El Movimiento

No cuenten pedazos
ni cuenten los fracasos
del movimeninto xicano
porque la historia sigue
y las victorias son muchas.

Cadenas los abrazos,
promesas en los vasos
de sueños y cerveza
bañando la poesía
inspirando la muralla
en la pared de la esquina.

Mas hoy los culatazos
antes de los balazos
en el estado de Chiapas
recuerdan que el movimiento
se ha cambiado de casa
a la opresión más vecina.

Cargan con nuevos plazos
y jalan fuertes lazos
los xicanos del nuevo milenio
con el mismo enemigo
y la causa es la de siempre,
dar dignidad a gente fina.

Also Published by Arte Público Press

Survival Supervivencia
Miguel Algarin
2009, ISBN: 978-1-55885-541-0, $16.95

The Other Man Was Me: A Voyage to the New World
Rafael Campo
1994, ISBN: 978-1-55885-111-5, $8.00

From the Cables of Genocide: Poems on Love and Hunger
Lorna Dee Cervantes
1991, ISBN: 978-1-55885-033-0, $7.00

Terms of Survival
Judith Ortiz Cofer
1995 (Second Edition), ISBN: 978-1-55885-079-8, $7.00

Woman, Woman
Angela de Hoyos
1996 (Second Edition), ISBN: 978-1-55885-156-6, $7.00

Selected Poetry
Cecilio García-Camarillo
2000, ISBN: 978-1-55885-281-5, $12.95

La Llorona on the Longfellow Bridge: Poetry y Otras Movidas
Alicia Gaspar de Alba
2003, ISBN: 978-1-55885-399-7, $11.95

Some Clarifications y otros poemas
Javier O. Huerta
2007, ISBN: 978-1-55885-500-7, $10.95

AmeRícan
Tato Laviera
2003, ISBN: 978-1-55885-395-9, $11.95

Un Trip through the Mind Jail y Otras Excursions
Raúl R. Salinas
1999, ISBN: 978-1-55885-275-4, $9.95

Thirty an' Seen a Lot
Evangelina Vigil-Piñón
1982, ISBN: 978-0-934770-13-2, $7.00

Borders
Pat Mora
1986, ISBN: 978-0-934770-57-6, $8.95

To order and for additional publications visit: www.artepublicopress.com

ML   3/12